THREAT

TO THE BODY

POLITIC

Foo Fighters to UAP

James P. Lough

THREAT TO THE BODY POLITIC
Foo Fighters to UAP

Editor: George Verongos

Hardback
ISBN: 9781736627211

DEDICATION

Senator Harry Reid
(1939–2021)
The Catalyst

In 2007, Senate Majority Leader Harry Reid, with the help of Senators Ted Stevens (R-AK) and Daniel Inouye (D-HI), added 22 million dollars to the Defense Intelligence Agency (DIA) budget to fund a five-year program to study UFOs. This modest expenditure started the Advanced Aerospace Threat Identification Program (AATIP). AATIP gathered sighting information, including the FLIR, Gimbal, and GOFAST naval aviation videos. These videos helped lead to today's growing UAP program. Thanks to Senator Reid's effort, we are poised to find answers to what may be the most significant revelation of the modern age.

Reid's foresight has led to inquiries into what has been hidden from the public and Congress for decades. With his choice of one Democrat and one Republican to co-sponsor his proposal, he started this quest off in a bipartisan manner that continues to this day. Senator Reid was a catalyst whose early efforts will help restore faith in our system of government and help explain how we fit into a larger reality. This book honors his memory and all his accomplishments for humanity.

CONTENTS

INTRODUCTION

Whatever you call them, Foo Fighters, Swedish Ghost Rockets, Flying Saucers, Green Fireballs, Unidentified Flying Objects, Unidentified Aerial Phenomena or Unidentified Anomalous Phenomena (UAP),[1] they have interacted with our military since World War II. Yet, how much our government actually understands has been as big a mystery as the phenomenon itself. To begin with, true UAP have defied our understanding, with their perplexing behavior and advanced technology. Our military's reaction has been equally perplexing. Over an 80-year history, the United States government's response has been a mix of passive-aggressive behavior primarily aimed at diminishing interest in the subject. Today, we are tantalizingly close to understanding the source and intent of whoever is behind these curious objects. Recent legislation has raised many questions about our military's knowledge of the phenomenon and how little of it has been shared with our elected civilian leadership. Currently, a third consecutive year of UAP legislation tries to learn from the past to assist today's understanding.

While most of this book's focus is on the past, it also discusses the current legislative efforts to understand UAP. The predominant legislative purpose is to see if these objects pose a danger to our aircraft as a navigation hazard or military threat. Experienced pilots, who have had encounters with these craft, have captured

---

[1] While the government now uses the term Unidentified Anomalous Phenomena (UAP), it appears to be the same phenomenon which has been seen for the last 80 years. The various terms for UAP will be used interchangeably depending on the context and time period being discussed. As to the use of the plural "phenomena" or the singular "phenomenon," this book assumes core UAP to be a single phenomenon. Lumping misidentified drones, balloons, and other mundane objects with core UAP obscures the true nature of the phenomenon. Whether the phenomenon has one or multiple sources, it is still likely a product of the same technological developments that, to date, seem beyond our grasp.

them on multiple sensors performing impossible aerobatics. Today's technology gives us a better window into the phenomenon not possible decades ago. Yet, incidents in our past show the same performance characteristics seen by aviators today. Is this the same phenomenon? If so, looking at the past can help us understand what is being seen today.

This book looks at our present struggles to understand this mystery. It also reviews past policies that show Congress is on the right track in its legislative efforts. Past UFO/UAP policies can help us better understand the policy choices of today. Using recently declassified records, this book explores key points in the public policy history of the UFO phenomenon. The period between 1947 and 1954 is particularly instructive. It was during this period that segments of the military and intelligence community set a course that largely continues to this day. The intent was to depress interest in the UFO phenomenon to keep it from becoming a public policy issue. What other activities lay behind these policies remains largely obscured. Today, government policies still contain many attitudes that extend back in time.

The book starts out with a discussion of today's UAP laws. For three consecutive years, Congress has proposed legislation aimed at enhancing our understanding of this mystery. Each legislative session has seen the adoption of stricter requirements intended to motivate the Department of Defense (DoD) and the 18 agencies of the intelligence community (IC) to cooperate. Working mostly behind closed doors, Congress continues to be at odds with the DoD and IC. The DoD/IC say they are concerned, but their actions tell a different story. For a large organization that can often be surprisingly nimble at addressing a new priority, the DoD has been slow to implement congressional policy.

This disconnect cannot be found with any other defense issue. Recent revelations show that many classified UAP-related programs will not allow oversight by national security committees.

It is more than a threat assessment. It involves a constitutional question about congressional oversight of these programs. A fundamental concern in a democracy. Should properly cleared civilian leaders chosen by the electorate have budgetary control over these programs? Congress believes they should.

After a discussion of today's legislation, the book looks at how recent actions by the DoD/IC undercut or delay the congressional UAP inquiry. Current responses have historical precedent, which is why yesterday matters today. Our look at the past begins with early actions taken to address the flying saucer phenomenon. They help explain many of today's perplexing reactions to congressional concerns.

By way of background, the book then reviews some of the challenges that America faced post-World War II. These challenges had a profound influence over the way the government addressed flying saucers. After WWII, our two largest allies, the Soviet Union and China, became our arch enemies. This situation had significant implications, leading to many excesses committed to preserve "our way of life" from the communist threat. The response to the flying saucer phenomenon borrowed tactics from the "Red Scare" to depress interest in the subject.

After the initial flying saucer craze, Air Force personnel noticed a post-1947 decline in civilian sightings. However, there was a concerning increase in flying saucer sightings around sensitive military facilities. By 1952, a dramatic increase in the numbers and quality of flying saucer sightings occurred across the country. This flying saucer "wave" included two July weekends of dramatic sightings over Washington, D.C. The combination of visual sightings confirmed by radar made national headlines. While damage control explanations disputed most radar confirmations, a large segment of the public was still concerned. President Truman asked the Central Intelligence Agency (CIA) to look into the matter. Working with the Air Force, the CIA eventually formed a scientific panel which spent four days studying the phenomenon and making recommendations to the incoming Eisenhower Administration.

This group of scientists reviewed a few cases selected by the CIA and learned about the "indirect" dangers of UFOs. The Robertson Panel issued a classified report with many findings outside of their scientific expertise. This book spends several chapters breaking down the Panel recommendations. In addition to finding that UFOs, as renamed by the Air Force, were not of scientific interest, they determined that, given enough information, UFOs were seen by people who were either (1) mistaken, (2) lying, or (3) delusional. The Panel's main "indirect" danger was that the Soviets would create a fake UFO invasion to mask a sneak attack. Since they found that all UFOs could be explained, none were a danger to national security. However, the CIA/Air Force claimed concern for a fake UFO invasion and the Panel accepted this recommendation. The Robertson Panel Report found that the public's interest in UFOs would "result in a threat to the orderly functioning of the protective organs of the body politic." Thereafter, policies were put in place to suppress interest in UFOs. The Panel's scientists also advised that certain UFO groups should be "watched" to prevent their "morbid" interest from spreading to the public.

Thereafter, several chapters are devoted to implementation measures employed by the Air Force and CIA. They show common tactics used to depress interest in the phenomenon. Most of the incidents are drawn from recently declassified documents. These examples raise legal concerns that echo abuses uncovered by a special Senate committee, during its 1970s investigation into illegal government conduct.[2]

The tactics used by the Air Force and CIA had constitutional implications. Free speech restrictions, property confiscation, and other similar tactics were commonplace. Several chapters go through the legal implications of the "debunking" program, including extralegal efforts to keep UAP information from Congress.

In the final two chapters, the focus is on what to make of the past UFO-related activities of the DoD/IC. First is a review of the psychological warfare efforts aimed at depressing interest in UFOs and how they impact today's oversight efforts. This psychological warfare campaign applied to a small group of people who were perceived as a threat to the "body politic." The final chapter contains thoughts about how the declassified record strongly indicates there was a long-term program to quietly manage the UFO "problem" away from the prying eyes of Congress. Much of today's resistance is a product of these efforts. The final chapter also addresses some of the challenges that arise from the sources of UAP, be they terrestrial or not. A bipartisan approach during a time of partisan turmoil has greatly assisted our ability to understand where we have been, how we address the challenges that arise, and how we will inform the public. Seldom does an issue held in such contempt for decades unite so many elected officials who agree on little else.

---

[2] Church Committee (U.S. Senate Select Committee on Intelligence Activities Within the United States), *Intelligence Activities and the Rights of Americans: 1976 U.S. Senate Report on Illegal Wiretaps and Domestic Spying by the FBI, CIA and NSA*, Red and Black Publishers (2007).

THREAT

TO THE BODY

POLITIC

Foo Fighters to UAP

CHAPTER ONE

TODAY'S UAP LEGISLATION

In 2007, a small appropriation for a five-year Pentagon UAP program, AATIP, started the ball rolling. Ten years later, on December 16, 2017, *Politico* and the *New York Times* revealed three declassified videos obtained by AATIP. The surprising Defense Intelligence Agency (DIA) release of FLIR, Gimbal, and GOFAST naval aviation videos raised serious questions about a phenomenon that has been highly classified, yet publicly derided.

Soon thereafter, members of the House and Senate Armed Services and Intelligence Committees started becoming impatient with the Pentagon's approach to UAP. In June 2020, Committee Chair Marco Rubio (R-FL) requested a report about UAP from the DoD and the Office of the Director of National Intelligence (ODNI). On June 25, 2021, Rubio received his response. The *Preliminary Assessment: Unidentified Aerial Phenomena* (*Preliminary Assessment*) raised more questions than it answered. The *Preliminary Assessment* contained little information about the 144 cases submitted during the study period, November 2004 to March 2021. Most of these cases were visual sightings, made by Navy aviators after a 2019 reporting program started. The majority of the sightings were confirmed by other electronic data. Based on the work of the Navy's Unidentified Aerial Phenomena Task Force (UAPTF), the report was supposed to be followed by an update on September 21, 2021, which never materialized, becoming an indicator of future intransigence.

While the *Preliminary Assessment* was being prepared in 2021, the House Armed Services Committee started drafting the FY2022

National Defense Authorization Act (NDAA). It contained the first UAP legislation in history. (50 United States Code (U.S.C.) §3373.) The 2022 NDAA was co-sponsored by the Armed Services Chair, Adam Smith (D-WA), and its Ranking Member, Mike Rogers (R-AL). For the UAP language, Chair Smith turned to Ruben Gallego (D-AZ). Rep. Gallego was the Chair of the Armed Services Subcommittee on Intelligence and Special Operations. He began work on a draft of the UAP language prior to receiving the *Preliminary Assessment*. On July 2, 2021, the chair and ranking member introduced House Resolution No. 4350 (NDAA), one week after the *Preliminary Assessment* was issued. This version of the defense bill contained language setting up a UAP program to replace the Navy's UAP Task Force. On September 23rd, the House voted 316-113 to approve H.R. 4350 and sent it to the Senate.

Once before the Senate, things got more interesting. With the release of the *Preliminary Assessment*, it was apparent that the members of the House and Senate Armed Services and Intelligence Committees were unimpressed by both the classified appendix and public version. During classified briefings, these committees had seen much clearer versions of FLIR, Gimbal, and GOFAST videos than the public and had briefings from pilots. Besides that, it appears that they had received a little more background information. Senator Mitt Romney (R-UT-Armed Services) and Senator Martin Heinrich (D-NM-Intelligence) both publicly stated that the briefings failed to show any serious possibility that UAP were created by a terrestrial adversary. The frustration over DoD's lack of urgency was echoed by Senator Kirsten Gillibrand (D-NY), who tweeted that we had to "take our heads out of the sand" about the potential threat caused by UAP.

Member concern was, in part, fueled by better public information than what Congress was receiving. Perhaps the best and most timely example came from former military personnel. On October 19, 2021, a press conference was hosted at the National Press Club by Air Force Captain (ret.) Robert Salas. Salas spoke of his own 1967 encounter with a UFO that shut down a flight of 10 intercontinental ballistic missiles. Also, several former Air Force personnel discussed similar experiences of ICBM interference by UAP. Author Robert Hastings also spoke about several incidents from his book, *UFOs and Nukes: Extraordinary Encounters at Nuclear Weapons Sites.* Within two weeks of the press conference, a significant UAP amendment to the defense bill was filed, including provisions to investigate nuclear-related incidents like those discussed at the press conference.

On November 4, 2021, Senator Kristen Gillibrand (D-NY)[3] submitted Senate Amendment 4281. Her amendment significantly revamped §1652 (later renumbered §1683), including mandatory annual UAP reporting requirements around nuclear facilities. On November 18, 2021, Gillibrand reintroduced her amendment but with four senate cosponsors, Marco Rubio (R-FL), Roy Blunt (R-MO), Martin Heinrich (D-NM) and Lindsey Graham (R-SC). Except for Graham, each were members of the Senate Select Committee on Intelligence. The addition of this bipartisan group of cosponsors significantly increased the amendment's profile. The Gillibrand amendment added mandates, including with whom the Pentagon was required to consult, what they were required to study, and how the new UAP office was funded.

While most of the language continues procedures placed in the original House Bill (HR 4350), this amendment contained stricter oversight provisions. For instance, if the UAP office is denied access to a classified program, notice of the denial must be given to chairs

---

[3] Senator Gillibrand was well suited to guide this new approach to UAP. She is one of a few senators that are on both the Senate Select Committee on Intelligence and the Senate Armed Services Committee. As an Armed Services Committee member, she has taken on tough issues that protect rank-and-file personnel. Most notably, the elimination of the military's "Don't ask, don't tell" policy and reforms to provide fairer procedural protections for military sexual assault claimants.

and ranking members of the House and Senate Armed Services and Intelligence Committees. This will help determine where information bottlenecks are located.

Five days after the amendment's reintroduction, Deputy Director of Defense Kathleen Hicks announced the replacement of the UAPTF with the Airborne Object Identification and Management Synchronization Group (AOIMSG). This new Pentagon UAP program had none of the oversight provisions in the NDAA. Issued while the Senate was considering the Gillibrand amendment, it was an unusual step. Essentially, it was an "end run" around the proposed congressional legislation. The timing of the hastily drafted AOIMSG policy was intended as an alternative to the proposed UAP law.

Another complication was the timing of the amendment and the limited time Congress had to act. If the UAP amendment was to be added at this stage, the entire defense bill would have to receive a new House vote, since it wasn't part of the House-approved version. For any differences between the Senate and House versions, the two approved versions usually go to a conference committee composed of members appointed by House and Senate leadership. This is how differences between the House and Senate versions are usually worked out. Once the conference committee agrees to the contents of the bill, the final version must be approved by both.

To avoid this dilemma, when the extra steps would also complicate other political concerns, a new approach was taken. Instead of using the time-consuming conference committee process, Senate leadership used a bill that had already been introduced to cut down the number of parliamentary steps. S. 1605 was chosen as the vehicle. This bill was originally authored by Senator Rick Scott (R-FL) to erect a memorial to the shooting victims of the Pulse Nightclub massacre. It had been signed by President Biden on June 25, 2021, on the tragic event's fifth anniversary. On December 7, 2021, congressional leadership agreed to reuse the bill to approve the Senate version of the NDAA and it was submitted to the House that day. This negotiated arrangement included the Gillibrand amendment with some new clarifying provisions. The NDAA was approved by the House 363-70. On December 15th, S. 1605 was approved by the Senate, 88-11. President Biden signed the bill on December 27, 2021. The approval rendered moot the Pentagon's AOIMSG program.

Overall, successive legislative actions got stricter over time. The June 2020 inquiry by the Senate Intel Committee was merely a request, not a mandatory law. After the *Preliminary Assessment* was distributed, it was apparent the involved members of Congress were becoming less confident in the DoD/IC approach to UAP. This led to a ratcheting up of the bill's UAP requirements. The UAP language grew from three subsections in the original version to 12 in the adopted final version.

The bill is now codified at Volume 50 United States Code §3373. §3373(a) (*Establishment of Office*) required that the UAP office be formed by June 25, 2022. The All-domain Anomaly Resolution Office (AARO) was eventually formed on July 20, 2022. Under §3373(b) (*Duties*), it has eight requirements, seven were in the original version, but with added specificity. For instance, the Gillibrand amendments, under §3373(b)(1), adds "adverse physiological effects" to the list of UAP-related issues to be analyzed.

The stronger mandates continued under §3373(c), *Response to and Field Investigations of Unidentified Aerial Phenomena.* It requires use of the best science available. The science first, policy continues under subsection §3373(d) (*Scientific, Technological, and Operational Analysis of Data on Unidentified Aerial Phenomena*), §3373(e) (*Data: Intelligence Collection*), §3373(f) (*Science Plan*) and §3373(g) (*Data; intelligence collection*). The purpose of the science plan is "develop and test, as practicable, scientific theories to ... account for characteristics and performance" of UAP and to "provide a foundation for potential future investments to replicate" UAP performance.

Subsection 3373(h) (*Annual Report*) contains one of three carryover subsections from the House version. It requires an annual report to congressional committees about the progress of the program. Each House and Senate Armed Services, Intelligence, Appropriations, and Foreign Policy Committees are to receive the annual report on or before October 31st through 2026.

The final three sub-parts under §3373(h)(2) were added by the Gillibrand amendment to understand UAP incidents around nuclear weapons facilities. §3373(h)(2)(M) requires an annual report on the number and type of incidents involving nuclear facilities. Under §3373(h)(2)(N), the annual report must consult with the Department of Energy Administrator for Nuclear Security about incidents involving the "production, transportation, or storage of nuclear weapons." The final nuclear-related sub-part (O) requires annual consultation with the chair of the Nuclear Regulatory Commission (NRC). The NRC regulates commercial nuclear power plants. The legislation requires the same kind of detail in semiannual congressional briefings. (§3373(i), *Semiannual Briefings*.) The last subsection is §3373(l), *Definitions*. The definition of UAP is expanded to include "transmedium objects or devices" and "submerged objects or devices." This addition is meant to include craft that can perform extraordinary maneuvers in the air, space, and underwater.

Overall, the fiscal year 2022 UAP legislative efforts became an iterative process. With each step, the requirements ratcheted up the types and amount of information provided on an ongoing basis. Senator Gillibrand's amendment tightens the UAP statutory mandates to address bureaucratic reluctance. The late DoD AOIMSG effort generated no support.

As Congress entered the second session of the 117th Congress in 2022, participating committee members continued to voice their displeasure at the pace and scope of efforts to implement the UAP legislation. This dissatisfaction was expressed in the July 2022 committee comments. Senate Intel Chair Mark Warner (D-VA) criticized the pace of UAP study as follows:

> "At a time when cross-domain transmedium threats to United States national security are expanding exponentially, the Committee is disappointed with the slow pace of DoD-led efforts to establish the office to address those threats and to replace the former Unidentified Aerial Phenomena Task Force as required in Section 1683 of the National Defense Authorization Act for Fiscal Year 2022. The Committee was hopeful that the new office would address many of the structural issues hindering progress."[4]

The referral of the FY2023 annual intelligence funding bill to the Senate floor contained further UAP study requirements, cosponsored by Senators Roy Blunt (R-MO), Marco Rubio (R-FL), Kirsten Gillibrand (D-NY) and Martin Heinrich (D-NM). It also required a historical compilation of UAP records. With this second round of legislative proposals, the core group of national security experts continued their efforts to gain the upper hand in this perplexing battle. The second consecutive UAP bill was eventually merged into the annual defense bill. This legislation requires the Pentagon and the intelligence community to gather information about secrecy agreements that prevent UAP witnesses from speaking about their experiences. Also, new UAP-related whistleblower protections will protect personnel who talk about their UAP-related experiences without retaliation. The legislation

---

[4] Senate Select Committee on Intelligence, Report 117–132: *Intelligence Authorization Act for Fiscal Year 2023*, Report together with additional views, July 22, 2022.

will also mandate a Government Accountancy Office (GAO) audit of AARO's efforts to study UAP since January 1945, including "any efforts to obfuscate, manipulate public opinion, hide, or otherwise provide incorrect unclassified or classified information about unidentified anomalous phenomena or related activities." (50 U.S.C. §3373(j)(1)(B)(ii)(III).)

The Senate Intel Committee's disappointment was bipartisan and unanimous. Few subjects have this unanimity in today's political environment. Also, having a second round of legislation during the same Congress (117th) on the same subject matter is a rare occurrence. Follow-up legislation usually occurs for curative purposes when technical errors need correction. Back-to-back legislation on the same subject matter usually reflects a fundamental policy disagreement between the legislative and executive branches. Yet, here, there was no noticeable policy disagreement between the White House and Congress. The White House did not lobby Congress to prevent the second round of UAP legislation. If the White House had no objection, who in the DoD/IC is creating the need for more legislation? As stated in the Intel Committee report issued to the Senate, the DoD and IC have deep "structural issues" that are preventing the implementation. The second legislative round during the same 117th Congress attempted to target these "structural issues."

Three different sections of the 2023 NDAA addressed UAP issues, §1673 (Unidentified Anomalous Phenomena Reporting Procedures), §6802 (Modification of Requirement for Office to Address Unidentified Anomalous Phenomena), and §6803 (Comptroller General of the United States Audits and Briefings on Unidentified Anomalous Phenomena Historical Record Report). Each section was intended to determine what we already know and why we are acting the way we are. Each also requires more access to current information by the national security oversight committees.

§1673 amends the reporting procedures established by the NDAA the year before. This section required a three-day notice to the chairs and ranking members of the national security committees, along with notice to congressional leadership, of programs that are not cooperating with the UAP investigation mandates. (FY2023 NDAA §1673(a)(4)(B).) Noncooperation includes the existence of any classified program that has not "been explicitly and clearly reported to the congressional defense committees or the congressional intelligence committees...." This requirement means that the Senate Committee on Intelligence is not being told everything about our UAP research programs.

§6802, *Modification of Requirement for Office to Address Unidentified Anomalous Phenomena*, names the UAP program the All-domain Anomaly Resolution Office (AARO) and makes mostly technical changes. Under 33 U.S.C. §3373(n)(1), the number of "appropriate congressional committees" who can receive classified UAP information was expanded by adding the House and Senate Appropriations, House and Senate Homeland Security Committees, Senate Committee on Commerce, Science, and Transportation, and House Committee on Science, Space, and Technology.

Lacking trust in the DoD/IC to investigate themselves, Congress added §6803 (Comptroller General of the United States Audits and Briefings on Unidentified Anomalous Phenomena Historical Record Report) which requires an audit of the UAP Historical Report prepared by AARO. The Comptroller General, head of the General Accountancy Office, shall give quarterly progress reports to AARO, with verbal reports on a semiannual basis to congressional national security committees and congressional leadership. The interest in the past is not merely academic. Similar sightings to today's Naval aviator videos have been reported by military aviators since 1942.

Overall, the first two rounds of UAP legislation opened up new avenues of study. The whistleblower provisions allowed personnel to come forward to reveal what is happening behind classified walls. These changes were followed up in the 118th Congress by more exacting requirements. In 2023, Congress is considering three legislative proposals for the 2024 fiscal year that are intended to eliminate continuing roadblocks. One is aimed at forcing secret programs either to lose funding or come under congressional oversight and budgetary control. Another sets up a process that will declassify most UFO/UAP documents. The third provision will fully fund the UAP program. This provision was necessary since the DoD did not fund AARO to the level required by the original UAP law adopted in 2021.

As this book goes to print, the legislative process to adopt new UAP provisions for fiscal year 2024 was still pending. The process has been complicated by the chaos in the House of Representatives that was temporarily operating without a Speaker and under a short-term continuing resolution to keep the government open. This dilemma may prevent approval of any legislation, let alone the UAP provisions. It could also create problems for bipartisan cooperation that has helped foster UAP legislation. Fortunately, the House and Senate cooperated on these provisions so, if the bipartisan cooperation is not sidetracked by larger political concerns, each of the three proposals should be included in the final versions of the NDAA and the Intel Bill. If not, the bills will slide into the 119th Congress and likely be reintroduced.

One FY2024 proposal supports AARO. For the first time, the UAP program will be fully funded. Leaving funding priorities to the DoD has left AARO unable to perform mandated tasks. These funding shortfalls have hampered its investigatory functions, particularly the requirement to investigate the historic responses to UAP. Since the beginning of the AARO program, testimony shows that AARO has only been able to extend its knowledge of UAP activities from 1998 to 1996. Adding two extra years of knowledge per year will mean that AARO will be looking at the post-WWII period around 2038. Efforts to learn about possible reverse engineering programs studying UAP, if left to the mid-level Pentagon officials, will never occur. This is why another way must be considered.

The legislation sunsetting any funding for secret UAP research projects will speed up the process of their disclosure. If adopted, it should expose improper spending in violation of federal contracting laws. In addition, the legislation to speed up release of classified UAP records would form a citizen committee to oversee the declassification of UAP records. This takes declassification authority away from the DoD and IC. The 25-year presumption that these documents must be disclosed unless the DoD/IC can meet a very high standard of proof turns the tables toward transparency. Both measures will help us see what our government has been doing about UAP since WWII.

The efforts to learn about hidden UAP research projects could help explain today's reticence to cooperate with Congress on this vital subject. It is a rare issue that Congress must go through three rounds of legislation to get the attention of the bureaucracy. Unless a Presidential administration is in a political war with Congress, one never sees this kind of pushback. Neither the Trump, nor the Biden Administration, pushed back on congressional UAP interest. None of the Defense Secretaries since 2017 have spoken against UAP legislative priorities. Upper level management of the DoD and IC have continued to claim they are cooperating. Yet, unclassified information is less revealing today than it was in 2021 under UAPTF.

The congressional legislative strategy is designed to accomplish two goals. First, to keep the two political parties on the same page. Second, the public records and the reverse engineering legislation are both aimed at taking discretion away from the DoD/IC. Noncooperation on mandated records and program disclosures will soon result in violations of the law. Faced with these new requirements, it is hoped that most, if not all, will comply with these mandates. However, considering the 70 plus years that this mystery has been kept away from Congress, there are bound to be efforts to escape compliance.

Changing locations of these secret programs; accelerating research using environmentally hazardous methods; hiding recovered UAP materials and records; and legal claims of ownership of materials actually recovered by the federal government are all likely methods to avoid losing control of these valuable assets. However, considering that many programs will involve contractors who have ongoing business with the federal government, such extralegal moves could affect the long-term bottom line of some large, multinational corporations. The records legislation will accelerate the declassification of UAP/UFO documents, including photographic evidence. While there is a House version, the Senate amendment is sponsored by a bipartisan group of Senate Majority Leader Chuck Schumer (D-NY), with Senators Mike Rounds (R-SD), Marco Rubio (R-FL), and Gillibrand (D-NY). The amendment establishes a citizen commission to review UAP/UFO documents. The proposed law presumes that any document older than 25 years is automatically declassified unless, by clear and convincing evidence, there is a reason that it should not be declassified. This significant provision means that a UAP record must be disclosed to the public unless a nine member citizen committee believes that the agency holding the document proves, by the toughest standard under civil law, that it must remain classified. Very few documents should meet this standard. Sponsorship by the Senate Majority Leader is significant. Legislative majority leaders of any party rarely, if ever, sponsor legislation. An indication of the bill's political importance. Unfortunately, the House rejected inclusion of the bipartisan records bill provisions calling for an independent reviewing body. The provisions of the House UAP records bill were adopted without this independent review procedure.

The full funding bill will give AARO the ability to meet legislative mandates. AARO has been underfunded by the DoD for two years despite 2021 legislation requiring funding. One result of lack of funding is that AARO delegated to the Air Force the job of reviewing the historical records about UFO/UAP activities. It is like putting the prime suspect in charge of its own investigation. The funding bill should fix that situation.

With all these moving parts, there will not be a rapid disclosure of what has been going on behind the scenes. If adopted, each provision will take time to implement. The reverse engineering disclosure law will take until late June 2024 before Congress has any information needed to make budgetary decisions. There will likely be recalcitrant defense contractors who will fight turning over information. The Records Declassification Committee will also require Senate confirmation of its nine members. It only takes one Senator to hold up the process of any nominee. The end of 2025 will probably be the soonest that records will begin to be released. The full funding bill will speed up some of AARO's work. However, how it sets priorities may not be readily apparent.

Each year, Congress has tightened standards in its search to understand who ultimately controls UAP research. Seldom, if ever, has Congress enacted legislation three years in a row to force the bureaucracy to comply with explicit legislative mandates. The source of this intransigence is still murky with top DoD and IC officials claiming to cooperate, while DoD/IC actions suggest otherwise. The DoD/IC response to this legislation will help us understand how much has changed from the decades of policies constructed without congressional input.

CHAPTER TWO

WHY YESTERDAY MATTERS TODAY

On December 16, 2017, three declassified videos forever changed the UFO/UAP debate. *Politico*[5] and the *New York Times* [6] published stories that released the FLIR, Gimbal, and GOFAST videos. Each showed objects performing maneuvers, without a visible means of propulsion, in a manner that defied conventional logic. It was unlike anything ever released by the military. The videos were declassified in August 2017 by the Defense Intelligence Agency (DIA). The declassification request was made by Luis (Lue) Elizondo, a soon to retire intelligence agent working in the Pentagon. Elizondo had worked with the AATIP UAP program, begun by a 2007 Senator Harry Reid (D-NV) appropriation.

Even though the videos were declassified, the Pentagon refused to approve public records requests for them. For example, in a January 27, 2020 response, the *Black Vault's* John Greenewald was denied records, including the FLIR video, because of national security concerns.[7] Freedom of Information Act (FOIA) requests for already public videos were denied on "national security" grounds

---

[5] https://www.politico.com/magazine/story/2017/12/16/pentagon-ufo-search-harry-reid-216111/.

[6] https://www.nytimes.com/2017/12/16/us/politics/unidentified-flying-object-navy.html.

[7] https://www.theblackvault.com/documentarchive/u-s-navy-denies-request-to-release-key-ufo-documents/.

until April 2020.[8] The 2017 release is still perplexing, considering DoD conduct before and after the release.

After 2017, the DoD went back to restricting access to similar incidents. Thereafter, some significant information did emerge. In June 2021, the *Preliminary Assessment* was released to Congress, as a public report with a classified appendix. After subtracting the cover page, glossary, and restatement of the Senate request, the document was only six pages long (2254 words). While it did not address most of the questions asked by Senate Intel, it made several significant revelations. Yet, its main importance was its mere existence. It was the first public U.S. government report that acknowledges there is an issue with UAP. Whether a national security or navigational threat, it admitted there is a potential threat. The *Preliminary Assessment* also made a number of significant observations about 143 out of 144 reports that could not be explained.

Even before its release, Congress went to work on the first UAP law. In response, ODNI failed to issue its promised September 21, 2021 UAP update. After the strong amendment was proposed on November 18, 2021 by Senator Kirsten Gillibrand, the Pentagon held a press conference on November 23rd to announce the formation of its own UAP program. Deputy Director of Defense Kathleen Hicks issued a short policy memorandum intending to establish a DoD program with the unwieldy acronym AOIMSG.[9] This proposed policy contained none of the legislative oversight provisions in the original House language or the subsequent Gillibrand amendment. The hastily drafted proposal was the bureaucracy's direct challenge to the UAP legislation.

---

[8] https://www.popularmechanics.com/military/research/a32289669/navy-official-release-ufo-videos/.

[9] https://www.defense.gov/News/Releases/Release/Article/2853121/dod-announces-the-establishment-of-the-airborne-object-identification-and-manag/.

It is a rare event when an agency makes a counterproposal during legislative debate. If the White House has a stake in the matter, such proposals are routine. However, the White House indicated no public support for the DoD proposal. It was announced by a deputy director, two days before Thanksgiving. The press release finished with the following statement: "In coming weeks, the Department will issue implementing guidance, which will contain further details on the AOIMSG Director, organizational structure, authorities, and resourcing."

In other words, DoD was still trying to figure out how this program was to be constituted. AOIMSG had no named director. All that was disclosed was a program with no oversight requirements. The scope of study was limited to certain geographic areas. The apparent goal was to stop the pending UAP legislation. Despite this proposal, the UAP legislation was approved without any organized congressional opposition. The first UAP law was signed by President Biden on December 27, 2021. The AOIMSG proposal became moot.

Later, during the second session (2022) of the 117th Congress, it became clear to members of the national security committees that the DoD and IC were taking their time to implement the new law. In signing the law, President Biden had issued a signing statement.[10] The statement raised concerns about congressionally mandated reports required under the FY2022 NDAA containing highly sensitive information. Citing four examples of congressional overreach, the Biden Administration made clear it will comply only if national security was not compromised. The NDAA UAP reporting provisions were not among the cited examples.

---

[10] https://www.whitehouse.gov/briefing-room/statements-releases/2021/12/27/statement-by-the-president-on-s-1605-the-national-defense-authorization-act-for-fiscal-year-2022/.

Once S. 1605 became law, there have been complaints about restriction of information. However, there hasn't been an instance where the Biden Administration used its concerns enumerated in its signing statement to stop any UAP information sharing with Congress. These complaints were aimed at the DoD/IC, not the President.

On May 17, 2022, the House Intelligence Subcommittee on Counterterrorism and Counterintelligence held the first UFO/UAP hearing since the July 29, 1968. The last hearing was before the House Committee on Science and Aeronautics (90th Congress, Second Session). That hearing was called a "Symposium on Unidentified Flying Objects." It took place just before the summer recess and two presidential-nominating conventions. A week after the symposium, the Republican Convention in Miami started, nominating Richard Nixon. Later, in August 1968, the Democrats met in Chicago amidst chaos and controversy. Coverage of the UFO hearing was quickly overtaken by news about the conventions and presidential race.

At the May 2022 hearing, a House Intelligence subcommittee heard from two witnesses, Undersecretary of Defense (Intelligence and Security) Ronald Moultrie and Office of Naval Intelligence (ONI) Deputy Director Scott Bray.[11] Undersecretary Moultrie oversees Pentagon intelligence agencies. Mr. Bray oversaw the Navy's UAP Task Force (UAPTF) as the ONI Deputy Director. They were the two main players, since the new UAP program had yet to appoint a director.[12]

---

[11] https://www.c-span.org/video/?520133-1/hearing-government-investigation-ufos.

[12] Just exactly when the UAP program director was appointed is unclear. At the hearing, Moultrie testified that a director had been appointed the day before, but did not name the director. Later, on July 20, 2022, Deputy Secretary of Defense Kathleen Hicks announced the appointment of Dr. Sean Kirkpatrick to

The May 17, 2022 hearing was started by Chair André Carson with a request that the UAP program refocus its efforts on the most concerning cases. Chair Carson stated that the UAP program was more concerned about finding answers to the simplest cases with mundane explanations, such as balloons, drones, and airborne clutter. He stated that Congress was more concerned about core UAP cases that perform unusual maneuvers, apparently without chemical propulsion. The Chair asked that the program devote more resources to troubling cases, including the 11 cases with near misses.[13] No commitment was made to pursue this strategy.

One commitment was made by Scott Bray. He testified that videos, like FLIR, Gimbal, and GOFAST, will no longer be publicly released to protect the "sources and methods" of intelligence gathering. No distinction was ever made between why the first three videos were declassified and further videos were being withheld. Interestingly, just prior to the hearing, there was a quick declassification of a video of a drone over the Black Sea being disabled by a Soviet MIG fighter jet. This video revealed far more sophisticated sensors than the three declassified UAP videos.[14] The video was in full color with very clear high-resolution picture quality, far beyond the grainy black and white videos declassified in 2017. Bray's statement about withholding any more UAP videos was later confirmed by the DoD. Undersecretary Moultrie testified about a commitment to openness and transparency. The UAP program had begun pulling back from its brief flirtation with transparency under the Navy's UAPTF.

---

head AARO. AOIMSG apparently came and went without a director, despite Moultrie's testimony to the contrary.

[13] *Preliminary Assessment: Unidentified Aerial Phenomena,* June 25, 2021, p. 6, https://www.c-span.org/video/?520133-1/hearing-government-investigation-ufos.

[14] https://www.cnn.com/2023/03/16/politics/us-military-video-drone-russian-jet/index.html.

The hearing had moments that make one question the effort of the DoD. Mr. Bray attempted to show a video of a fast moving UAP. Neither the audience nor the subcommittee was able to follow the presentation. Eventually, Bray gave up, as his laptop was unable to display the video in a recognizable form. Considering this was a presentation to Congress, one would expect that the audiovisual portion of the testimony would be practiced ahead of time. The attempt looked amateurish and demonstrated a lack of hearing preparation.

A lack of preparation was also demonstrated by the testimony. The two DoD personnel were unable to answer basic questions about the phenomenon. Undersecretary Moultrie stated that the records of the phenomenon held by the new UAP program only dated back to 1998. For a phenomenon with reports dating back to 1942 Army Air Corps flight records, the program's knowledge base showed a lack of depth and inquisitiveness. Congressman Mike Gallagher (R-WI) asked questions about a nuclear incident shutting down 10 ICBMs in 1967 at Maelstrom Air Force Base. Neither witness was aware of the incident. Considering the incident had been the subject of a recent Washington, D.C. National Press Club press conference about nuclear weapon/UAP encounters, one would think that the UAP program would have some awareness about this incident.

After the hearing, Congress continued moving forward with its second round of legislation. However, once the AARO program was constituted and had an appointed director, Dr. Sean Kirkpatrick, the delays continued.[15] As per UAP legislation, the first annual report was due on October 31, 2022. It was not filed until January 13, 2023. Even though it was over two months late, the extra time taken did not result in more data analysis. In fact, most of the details

---

[15] On July 15, 2022, the DoD renamed AOIMSG to the All-domain Anomaly Resolution Office (AARO), after the June 25th statutory deadline. On July 20, 2022, Hicks appointed Dr. Sean Kirkpatrick to head AARO.

found in the Navy's UAPTF 2021 *Preliminary Assessment* were not present in AARO's first annual report. While the total number of reports was listed, there was no real breakdown of their characteristics, except a marked increase in the number of reports that had mundane explanations. A majority of the reports were attributed to natural or man-made objects. There were 366 reports with 247 new reports and 119 holdover reports from the 2021 *Preliminary Assessment* reporting period.

The raw 2022 report numbers, however, gave very few clues of the types of encounters. We do not know how many near misses occurred; how many incidents were sightings showing unusual flight characteristics; how many incidents demonstrated propulsion without chemical propellants; how many unidentified sightings were captured both visually and by sensors; and whether any sightings were tracked by sensors before or after any visual sighting. Instead, the annual report's analysis concentrated on incidents that do not present any of these disturbing qualities. AARO's emphasis was not what was requested at the May 2022 hearing.

In the 2022 annual report, 195 reports had unremarkable explanations with 26 drones, 163 balloons and 6 reports of debris characterized as "clutter." Out of 366 reports in the 2022 annual report, AARO was able to increase the identified rate from the 2021 UAPTF rate of 0.7% to 53%. Quite a change that was never explained. Since the 2022 annual report included 119 reports from the 2021 *Preliminary Assessment*, the sudden increase in resolved cases from 2021 to 2022 defies explanation if the same criteria were applied to each report.

The 2022 annual report gave virtually no data about the unidentified cases. In the 2021 report, there were 80 out of 144 reports that had sensor confirmation of visual pilot reports. No data in the 2022 report was provided about the characteristics of the unknown 171 reports. An undefined number of these reports "demonstrated unusual flight characteristics or performance capabilities, and require further analysis." The 2021 report mentioned 21 of 143 incidents listed as unknown, which displayed unusual flight characteristics. In the 2022 annual report, all we are told is that some cases demonstrated extraordinary capabilities. However, the latest report showed that military aviators apparently failed to identify 162 more balloons than in the first report. Either military pilots were having more trouble identifying balloons, or the ODNI/AARO collaboration failed to disclose a drastic shift in how AARO analyzes UAP reports.

The newest report probably reflects a change in how the military analyzes UAP, without saying so. This change takes the AARO further away from the intent of Congress. The 2021 report discussed the safety hazard found in 11 reported near misses out of 144 reports. The 2022 annual report only mentions that there were no collisions between military aircraft and UAP. We are left to speculate as to how many aircraft had dangerously close passes. The 2022 annual report is hardly reassuring to a Congress concerned about the frequency of near misses.

The same reluctance to provide information contained in the 2021 report was true for UAP that exhibited "unusual UAP movement patterns or flight characteristics." In the 2021 *Preliminary Assessment*, there were 21 reports of 18 incidents where objects performed maneuvers impossible by even our modern high-performance aircraft. The 2022 annual report contained no breakdown of reports with unusual UAP movement patterns or flight characteristics. This concern was highlighted at the May 17, 2022 House Committee on Intelligence Subcommittee hearing about UAP. AARO ignored the congressional request to concentrate on the most concerning cases. Instead, AARO emphasized the "low hanging fruit" that have mundane explanations.

Looking at the 2022 annual report, it is difficult to figure out the reason for a 74-day delay. The 12-page report was short on analysis and filled with background information. The cover, table of contents and appendix made up six pages. The appendix contained generic program information, including a glossary and three pages of statutory language applicable to the UAP program. The actual analysis was limited to 555 words.

The assessment period ended on August 30, 2022, two months before the 2022 annual report's publication deadline. Apparently, there were no glitches causing the delay. In response to a FOIA request about the delay, there were no reported documents informing Congress that the initial report would be late. The response to the FOIA request reads, in part, as follows:

> "After a thorough search of our records and databases, no records responsive to your request were located. As the annual report is written with data and support from the Department of Defense, coordination required additional time. The report is currently undergoing the normal and appropriate approvals process before it is delivered to Congress."[16]

The crux of this letter is that no correspondence was sent to Congress, informing them of the delay. Yet, it took more than two months for ODNI to minimally comply with the statutory requirement. The excuse was that ODNI needed to coordinate with the Pentagon, something that was known ahead of time. In the first of only five annual reports required by Congress, the first annual report left out important information found in the 2021 *Preliminary Assessment*. The data left out would show UAP impact on aircraft safety. Supplying data of the sort previously disclosed would not impact any classified sources or methods. Sharing this general

---

[16] ODNI FOIA case no. DF-2023-00028 (December 5, 2022).

statistical data is the bare minimum required to educate the public on an issue that was important enough for Congress to approve multiple rounds of legislation. We are left with the impression that the purpose of this delay is to run out the clock on the five-year annual report requirement.

Another way to look at the intent of DoD is to see the activities it undertook during the delay. AARO said nothing to explain the reasons for the delay. It made no public statement to explain, even at its Media Day (press conference). However, news reports around the time of the 2022 report's deadline mentioned that it was "expected this week."[17] Similar stories talked about it being out by the end of November. Each story, mostly from traditional defense reporters, talked about the report being issued "soon."

During this delay, AARO held a December 16, 2022 press conference with DoD spokesperson Susan Gough, Undersecretary Ronald Moultrie, and AARO Director Dr. Sean Kirkpatrick in attendance. When asked about the number of cases in the 2022 annual report, it took several follow-up questions to get the officials to admit that there were "several hundred" reports. Dr. Kirkpatrick stated:

> "I don't want to get ahead of the next report when it comes out. So, when that comes out, you'll get a better idea of what our batting average is."[18]

The answer left it to the release of the 2022 annual report issuance. However, no press conference was held after its release.

---

[17] *i.e.,* ABC News, "Another UFO report expected this week, some incidents still unexplained," October 31, 2022, https://abcnews.go.com/Politics/ufo-report-week-incidents-unexplained/story?id=92303931.

[18] DoD, "Media Roundtable on the All-domain Anomaly Resolution Office," December 16, 2022, https://www.defense.gov/News/Transcripts/Transcript/Article/3249303/usdis-ronald-moultrie-and-dr-sean-kirkpatrick-media-roundtable-on-the-all-domai/.

This limited questions about its contents. There was no forum where questions could be asked about its lack of data or whether the methodology had changed.

During the delay, DoD had been the source of several articles that downplayed the contents of the yet-to-be-issued report. One common element in most of these news reports was the use of the term "enthusiast" to describe people with an interest in the UAP policy issue.[19] The use of the term "enthusiast" harkens back to the early years of the UFO phenomenon when the official CIA UFO history began by calling people who had an interest in the subject "UFO buffs."[20] Both terms suggest a less-than-serious interest in a subject unworthy of public policy consideration. Some of these articles went further, stating that UFO "enthusiasts" will be "disappointed" the "soon to be issued" report will not disclose that aliens are visiting the planet. This pattern of identical degrading language popping up in several articles about the same topic indicates the DoD/IC spokespersons still use derogatory descriptions that perpetuate the stigma surrounding the UAP subject.

It likely was a term used by Pentagon officials unless reporters from several news outlets independently decided to use it. This is not the first time that DoD officials have used demeaning terms to describe those interested in the phenomenon. Despite claims that the Pentagon is trying to destigmatize discussion of UAP, it appears that condescending descriptions are once again used to describe those interested in the phenomenon. It appears that derogatory descriptions and misleading time estimates were used in

---

[19] *i.e.* Reuters, "Latest U.S. defense-intelligence report on UFOs to be made public soon," November 3, 2022, https://www.reuters.com/world/us/latest-us-defense-intelligence-report-ufos-be-made-public-soon-2022-11-04/.

[20] Haines, Gerald K. "CIA's Role in the Study of UFOs, 1947–90 (A Die-Hard Issue)," https://www.cia.gov/resources/csi/studies-in-intelligence/studies-in-intelligence-1997/cias-role-in-the-study-of-ufos-1947-1990/.

discussions with reporters that are seen as allies of the DoD/ODNI narrative. This is very similar to press conduct concerning the late 1960s UFO study by the University of Colorado "Condon" Committee. The Air Force sponsored study had support from many friendly journalists. Most significant was the support of the *New York Times* science editor, Walter Sullivan, who wrote the foreword to the publication of the committee's study, playing the role of advocate, not journalist. The Condon study helped the Air Force put an end to its public-facing study of UFOs.

Soon after release of the 2022 annual report, the country was gripped with a saga about the journey of a Chinese spy balloon.[21] Eventually, three other objects were discovered in U.S. and Canadian airspace.[22] The three objects were also shot down but never recovered. After the discovery of the Chinese spy balloon, the military stated that it had adjusted sensors to look for these objects.[23] The adjustments to sensors picked up objects that were not seen before. This raises questions about the surge of balloons in the 2022 annual report. Each report was made prior to multiple DoD statements about when the "adjustment" of sensors occurred. Therefore, the sensor adjustments in late January 2023 could not have played a part in the exponential increase in solved cases.

On April 19, 2023, the Chinese spy balloon incident was followed up by an appearance of AARO Director Sean Kirkpatrick before Senate Armed Services Subcommittee on Emerging Threats and Capabilities. After appearing in closed session, Kirkpatrick

---

[21] https://www.cnn.com/2023/02/02/politics/us-tracking-china-spy-balloon/index.html.

[22] https://www.nytimes.com/article/ufo-object-balloon-shot-down.html.

[23] https://www.npr.org/2023/02/14/1156740596/chinese-balloon-priority-sensors-military-salvage-south-carolina.

participated in a short open session. His opening statement included the following:

> "I want to underscore today that only a very small percentage of UAP reports display signatures that could reasonably be described as 'anomalous.' The majority of unidentified objects reported to AARO demonstrate mundane characteristics of balloons, unmanned aerial systems, clutter, natural phenomena, or other readily explainable sources. While a large number of cases in our holdings remain technically unresolved, this is primarily due to a lack of data associated with these cases. Without sufficient data, we are unable to reach defendable conclusions that meet the high scientific standards we set for resolution, and I will not close a case that we cannot defend the conclusions of."

Kirkpatrick did not explain how AARO found a radically different mix of objects compared to what the UAP Task Force reported. The AARO Director discounted unexplained cases by stating that it was "primarily due to a lack of data associated with these cases." This explanation is curious since 80 of the 143 unexplained cases in the 2021 UAPTF report had visual confirmation supported by sensor data. In the AARO 2022 annual report, there is no breakdown showing how many unexplained cases had sensor data to back up the visual reports. AARO has never explained what data is lacking that differentiates the 2021 Navy report from the 2022 AARO report. Instead, he paints a broad brush to cast doubt on hundreds of unexplained cases without explaining what data was needed. In the 2021 report, 14.5% of cases exhibited truly anomalous behavior, most having visual sightings confirmed by sensor data. There is no similar breakdown in the AARO 2022 report.

As will be seen, a lack of data was used to explain away difficult cases during the Air Force Project Bluebook Era (1952–1970). The CIA 1953 Robertson Panel also found that "unknowns" would be solved if there was more data. Yet, there was never a breakdown of what data would be needed to help in both eras. The generic "lack of data" excuse does not explain what is missing and how to fix it. Instead, the claim, yesterday and today, is that the unknowns will turn into solved cases with undefined "missing data" supplying the answers.

One possibility is that AARO could be including 119 solved cases that were not included in the 2021 *Preliminary Assessment*. Adding solved cases to the 2022 AARO numbers would boost the number of mundane cases. In turn, it would dramatically boost AARO's "batting average." Regardless of how they did it, AARO's solved rate is hard to explain since AARO did not provide the data behind its analysis. They only used 555 words to explain their findings. The bottom line is that AARO did not heed a congressional request to take cases with simple explanations out of the AARO system.

The frustration over AARO's lack of transparency has led to the emergence of a new player in the UAP inquiry. The House Oversight and Accountability Committee Chair James Comer announced it would hold a UAP hearing before the summer recess.[24] This announcement was made while several UAP bills were being considered for the 2024 fiscal year.

On July 26, 2023, the House Oversight and Accountability Subcommittee on National Security, the Border, and Foreign Affairs held an unclassified hearing on UAP. It featured three witnesses, two former Navy fighter pilots, and a defense intelligence officer. Witness Navy Lt. Ryan Graves was a carrier pilot who witnessed

---

[24] https://www.salon.com/2023/06/08/uap-whistleblower-ufo-non-human-intelligence-comer-congress-dod/.

multiple UAP while stationed on the U.S.S. *Theodore Roosevelt* during 2014-15. He was involved in a dramatic near miss with an unknown object while entering a training area off the East Coast. The object flew between two fighters, while in close formation. After retirement, Graves became the Executive Director of Americans for Safe Aerospace. A military pilot-led nonprofit organization focused on UAP air safety issues. Former Navy Commander David Fravor also testified. He was an F/A-18 pilot who commanded a flight squadron on the U.S.S. *Nimitz* during the November 2004 UAP incidents. He was a witness of a "tic-tac" UAP off the coast of San Diego. Fravor is on the Aircrew Leadership Council of Americans for Safe Aerospace. Graves and Fravor both spoke about their UAP incidents and opined that the objects they encountered could not have been a product of terrestrial manufacture.

The third witness, David Grusch, was assigned to the UAPTF to search for hidden UAP programs. He filed a whistleblower complaint alleging harassment resulting from inquiries during his UAPTF assignment as a detailee from the National Geospatial-Intelligence Agency (NGA). The IC Inspector General considered his complaint to be "urgent and credible" and informed congressional intel committees about it in July 2022. While his whistleblower complaint alleged adverse treatment because of his inquiries into secret UAP reverse engineering programs, the complaint did not discuss his findings related to secret UAP programs. The congressional hearing gave him a chance to discuss, under oath, some of what he learned from personnel who had direct knowledge of secret UAP research programs.

However, Grusch was unable, in the unclassified setting, to report details of his discoveries. Many of the subcommittee members on the Republican side of the aisle claimed sinister motives for not having access to classified UAP information. However, the reason for the lack of access was statutory. When the 117th Congress adopted the first two rounds of UAP legislation, the language limited the number of committees that are "appropriate" to receive classified UAP information.[25] House Oversight was never listed as one of the 12 "appropriate" committees. An overwhelming bipartisan majority voted to approve this limitation.

The hearing itself was remarkable for reasons unrelated to the actual phenomenon being studied. Most important was the level of bipartisanship displayed. During the 118th Congress, the House Oversight Committee has been one of the most partisan committees. Their ups and downs are great fodder for the 24-hour news cycle we live in. While bipartisanship is often boring, it was refreshing to see this subcommittee act in a bipartisan manner. With very few slipups, the conduct of the hearing stayed within a largely unified approach. Even inviting in non-subcommittee members to participate did not change the tone. Apart from Rep. Virginia Foxx (R-NC) spending her five minutes of time bashing the Biden Administration about the 2023 Chinese balloon incident, there were few flashes of partisan rancor. A far cry from the Hunter Biden/Impeachment Inquiry focus that has played a prominent role in much of the Oversight Committee's work. The hearing was a testament to the lack of partisan rancor associated with this subject.

Another unusual aspect of the hearing was the reaction from the AARO Director to whistleblower testimony. Post-hearing, Director Kirkpatrick wrote a LinkedIn post about the hearing. Kirkpatrick acknowledged it was written by him in his personal capacity. The post attacks Mr. Grusch, claiming that he was never detailed to AARO. Instead, he had been assigned to UAPTF, AARO's predecessor, by the NGA. In his LinkedIn post, AARO Director Kirkpatrick also claims that Grusch did not uncover evidence of programs that have been reverse engineering UAP.[26]

---

[25] 50 U.S.C. §3373(n)(1).

[26] https://www.metabunk.org/threads/statement-by-aaro-head-sean-kirkpatrick-on-the-hoc-uap-hearing.13069/.

Kirkpatrick also challenged the House Oversight Subcommittee for holding the hearing without briefing AARO. He further argued that the subcommittee hearing and the Grusch testimony impugned the integrity of the personnel of AARO.[27] The post, accurate or not, was a stinging rebuke of a congressional subcommittee and an employee who had filed a whistleblower complaint. Regardless of the veracity of the Grusch testimony, the publishing of this letter was a highly significant departure from government protocols. Kirkpatrick's post was followed up with a statement by Pentagon spokesperson Susan Gough. Gough reiterated that Kirkpatrick was speaking in his own capacity and not as the AARO Director. She further stated that AARO has no evidence of any hidden programs claimed by Grusch in his testimony.

Both the Kirkpatrick and the Hicks statements limit the claims of "no such knowledge" to AARO alone. Despite press reports to the contrary, neither claimed that the DoD or IC are completely unaware of any reverse engineering programs. The lack of knowledge of any hidden programs is limited to AARO, an underfunded, recently constituted program. Neither the Kirkpatrick post nor the Hicks statement actually rule out the possibility that such programs exist. There is no mention that "after a diligent search" AARO has not found evidence of such programs. Currently, the legally required historical review of our UAP-related history is ongoing. Also, Kirkpatrick does not mention that AARO ever reached out to House Oversight Committee Chair James Comer after he announced the intention of the Oversight Committee to hold a UAP hearing. Since its subcommittee was not authorized to receive classified briefings, an outreach effort from AARO would have been appropriate.

---

[27] https://apnews.com/article/congress-ufos-uaps-pentagon-aliens-631ad4d174ee9559580935ec11afcf3f; https://thedebrief.org/director-of-pentagons-uap-investigations-challenges-claims-made-in-recent-uap-hearing/.

Instead, the AARO Director leveled a personal attack at the Oversight Subcommittee. While Kirkpatrick recognized the right of the Oversight Subcommittee to conduct a hearing, he failed to take steps, in his official capacity, to discuss the status of AARO's investigation of the matter with the subcommittee. This instance of trying to throw mud into the gears of congressional oversight is reminiscent of earlier Pentagon and CIA attempts to divert Congress from oversight into UAP issues.

Kirkpatrick's handling of the matter was outside the bounds of normal government discourse. While government employees retain free speech protections to speak out about issues of public concern, there are judicially established limitations to public employee speech. They cannot engage in public speech if it interferes with their government job.[28] Working with Congress is part of the AARO Director's job. Speaking out interfered with Kirkpatrick's job duties. The problem caused by his post raises larger concerns. It raises a constitutional issue. As previously discussed, civilian control of the military is required under a number of clauses in the Constitution.[29] The matter in dispute involves whether there are programs being hidden from Congress. Congress has an absolute right to investigate claims that government funds have been improperly diverted for an unknown purpose. The Senate Select Committee on Intelligence, with whom Kirkpatrick claims to have a good working relationship, has proposed legislation to force hidden programs to comply with new legislative requirements. The Senate Intel Committee has referred this proposal to the Senate floor by a 17-0 vote. Without having finished conducting a diligent search for these programs, Kirkpatrick has criticized a congressional committee for making an inquiry. Kirkpatrick stated: "AARO has yet to find any credible evidence to support the

---

[28] *Heffernan v. City of Paterson*, 578 U.S. 266, 270 (2016).

[29] https://crsreports.congress.gov/product/pdf/IF/IF11566.

allegations of any reverse engineering program for non-human technology."[30] "Yet" is the operative word. AARO is still looking, but has prejudged Grusch's claims because it did not pass through AARO first.

In his post, Kirkpatrick has mentioned that law enforcement is part of the AARO program. A more appropriate method of raising his concerns that whistleblower Grusch was fabricating claims in sworn testimony would be a referral to the Justice Department to investigate. Instead, in a fit of pique, he handled the matter as a private citizen in a way that complicates his role as AARO Director.

The question of whether Grusch is telling the truth did not start with his congressional testimony. He had filed a whistleblower complaint with the Intelligence Community Inspector General. While the actual complaint only alleges retaliation for making inquiries about classified UAP programs, the IG forwarded it to the Senate Select Committee on Intelligence in July 2022 with a finding that the complaint was "urgent" and "credible."[31] One assumes that the IG performed some level of due diligence before making the required findings for delivery of the complaint to House and Senate Intel. At a minimum, the IG would have verified his assignment that led to the alleged harassment. Another whistleblower who was accused of not holding a position involving UAP issues was Luis Elizondo. Elizondo posted in social media that Grusch was a credible source of information and mentioned his assignment to the UAP Task Force, a predecessor to AARO.

---

[30] https://apnews.com/article/congress-ufos-uaps-pentagon-aliens-631ad4d174ee9559580935ec11afcf3f; https://thedebrief.org/director-of-pentagons-uap-investigations-challenges-claims-made-in-recent-uap-hearing/

[31] https://www.unknowncountry.com/headline-news/ic-inspector-general-deems-uap-recovery-whistleblowers-claims-credible-and-urgent/.

The circumstances of the Elizondo AATIP UAP program assignment sounds similar to Grusch's situation.[32] Both were intelligence personnel assigned to UAP programs. Both found evidence about UAP that contradicted the narrative of the DoD and IC. Both had alleged harassment and filed whistleblower complaints. Both had Susan Gough, a DoD spokesperson, deny their UAP assignments.[33] Both had others verify their assignments. In Elizondo's case, former Senate Majority Leader Harry Reid verified his AATIP assignment.

Later, on October 17, 2023, AARO made public its 2023 annual report.[34] It is the first action taken by AARO before a statutory deadline (October 31st). However, the report only covered eight months, August 31, 2022 to April 30, 2023. The timing of the report issuance was discussed at an earlier Senate subcommittee hearing. At the April 19, 2023 Senate Armed Services Subcommittee on Emerging Threats and Capabilities hearing, Kirkpatrick promised that the 2023 report would be out within two to three months of the hearing:

> "Our next annual report you all have given us— moved it up to June, July—we are going to be having that done about that timeframe and we will have a— we will be combining a whole number of reports into that one."

The reason for delay from the promised date is not known. AARO's second annual report mostly talked about promised

---

[32] https://www.politico.com/news/2023/07/28/pentagon-ufo-boss-congress-hearing-00108822.

[33] https://www.theblackvault.com/documentarchive/pentagon-reinforces-mr-luis-elizondo-had-no-responsibilities-on-aatip-senator-harry-relbid-2009-memo-changes-nothing/.

[34] https://www.aaro.mil/Portals/136/PDFs/FY23_Consolidated_Annual_Report_on_UAP-Oct_2023.pdf?ver=BmBEf_4EBtMRu9JZ6-ySuQ%3d%3d.

changes in procedures and analytical methods which, if implemented, will give AARO more tools. While process updates formed the majority of new information in the report, the emphasis on incidents with mundane performance characteristics continued. This reflects a consistent pattern. Objects with ordinary flight characteristics consume most of the analysis in the report. Little or no information is provided about anomalous objects that have no explanation, except to hint that sensor errors must be the cause.

Congress has come to understand that it cannot rely on AARO either to meet statutory deadlines or deliver a fully complete end product when promised. Virtually every date, either promised or mandated by law, has been missed since the report issued by the Navy's UAPTF. The 2021 *Preliminary Assessment* was filed on the promised date. For the first AARO report to have been filed on time, AARO had to cut four months off the annual reporting period. The current AARO approach still appears to be drawing lessons from the past. Delays were common and often used to buy time until the fervor of the moment passed.

The 2023 annual report had 291 reports, with 274 reports during the eight-month reporting period for an average of 34.5 reports per month, most limited to four military operations areas worldwide. The overall totals included 17 reports from the 2019–2021 period when the Navy started their formal reporting program, and an Air Force six-month pilot program added a small number of cases. For the first time, the FAA contributed 100 reports from U.S. territory and adjacent waters. The 2023 report has no breakdown of the types of reports or their characteristics. AARO continues its practice of not explaining the behavior of any true UAP, as the case breakdown found in the 2020 UAPTF *Preliminary Assessment*.

One thing is clear. The focus is still on the simplest cases. For instance, AARO is helping establish a training program based on data collected from reports showing mundane objects such as balloons. While this may help lower the number of balloon misidentification cases, it will not prepare pilots for confronting truly anomalous phenomenon. There was also a case study of one incident showing an object that turned out to be an airliner. Yet, there was no follow up information about any cases that could not be explained as a traditional object.

This report used two charts, but neither chart gave any information that could shed light on the types of cases drawing congressional concern. A chart showed the altitude of most sightings without explanation of the type of sightings being categorized. It only helped show the altitudes of the pilots reporting the conduct. A pie chart was also included that described the shapes of objects reported. Of objects with a distinctive shape, orbs were the most common with 25% of the sample. The chart did nothing to explain the flight characteristics of the different object types. The various shapes reported mimicked UFO reports for the history of the phenomenon.[35] One orb video was shown at the April 19, 2023 Senate subcommittee hearing that was misidentified in the report as occurring on March 17, 2023. The use of this orb video is the only anomalous object released by the DoD since the declassification of the three 2017 videos (FLIR, Gimbal, and GOFAST).

As with the 2022 report, the emphasis remains on the "low hanging fruit" and not the concerning cases displaying anomalous behavior like the 2004 *Nimitz* "tic-tacs." Just months before the report issuance, Lt. (ret.) Ryan Graves testified under oath to a congressional subcommittee that an orb inside a cube-shaped object was waiting for him and his wingman as they entered a classified control access point to a training area off the Atlantic

---

[35] *i.e.* National Investigations Committee on Aerial Phenomenon (NICAP), Richard H. Hall (Editor), *The UFO Evidence*, (1964), reprint Barnes & Noble Books (1997). A full copy of this book is in the CIA UFO archives. https://www.cia.gov/readingroom/docs/CIA-RDP81R00560R000100010001-0.pdf.

coast. As the two planes entered the training area in a tight formation, the cube flew between the planes in a high-speed pass. This type of encounter, seen visually by the pilots, when confirmed by sensors, could not be the product of "sensor error."

Overall, the latest conduct by the DoD and IC harkens us back to the Project Blue Book days with its fervor to hype "solved" cases and downplay the perplexing ones. Also, the "stigma" that anyone faced in the military attached to the UFO/UAP subject matter is present in both eras. The Grusch criticism fits this pattern. For all of the claims of transparency, the DoD has been dialing back information provided to the public. All the while, they are delaying steps required by law. These delays will have a twofold impact. First, the emphasis on cases with simple explanations takes center stage. At the same time, cases that show the most potentially threatening capabilities are hardly discussed. This study method puts off consideration of the hard truths surrounding cases like Graves and Fravor witnessed. Second, the continued delays in implementing the five-year reporting program to Congress are running out the clock. Ignoring statutory deadlines are attempts to ensure that the mystery will continue. These tactics appear to have their origins in the Air Force/CIA collaboration, discussed in the following chapters.

With all these moving parts, it is unlikely there will be a quick disclosure about what is going on behind the scenes. If adopted, each provision in the pending 2024 fiscal year legislation will take time to implement. The reverse engineering disclosure law will take until the summer of 2024 before Congress has information needed to make budgetary decisions about these hidden programs. There will likely be recalcitrant defense contractors that will fight turning over their information. The end of 2025 will probably be the soonest that records will begin to be released. The full funding bill will speed up some of AARO's work. However, how they set priorities with this funding infusion may take a while to become apparent.

As this book goes to press, bipartisanship in the face of these bureaucratic headwinds continued. National security committees and bipartisan leadership have opted for closer cooperation. Congress is taking a two-pronged approach with bills that have companion versions in the House and Senate. With the adoption of the FY2024 National Defense Authorization Act, UAP amendments will be present. This process required some changes, most notably, the House version of the UAP records bill was adopted without containing the independent review panel. This leaves each agency holding the UAP records will be in charge of the declassification process. Senate leaders have vowed to push for an independent panel review process for the FY2025 NDAA. So the UAP legislative process had some setbacks due to partisan issues in the House on the Republican side.

The past can inform us about the reasons for today's unusual behavior. Looking at the past provides a window into the rationale behind today's dichotomy. UAP have historically been of no publicly acknowledged concern, but are still hidden behind classified walls, even kept from Congress. People with an interest in the subject have been denigrated as "flying saucer buffs" or "enthusiasts" while basic records about the subject are still highly classified. High-resolution, color drone footage is quickly available for public viewing if they show a Russian jet interfering with our drones. Yet, it takes years to gain the release of fuzzy black and white videos of UAP. The official position of AARO is that "unknowns" can be eliminated if more data was available. This same explanation has been given for decades. Since the 1940s, a tight lid has been put on release of information for a phenomenon that has been officially "not a threat to national security."

AARO also has consistently discounted the most puzzling cases, showing anomalous phenomenon, by claiming a lack of data. As this book was going to press, AARO's Director Sean Kirkpatrick amplified this rationale of only concentrating on current cases while ignoring the history of UAP pilot reports. Specifically, he focused on the lack of data from the 2004 U.S.S. *Nimitz* "tic-tac" incidents.[36] He stated that electronic records were not available for AARO to review this incident. The October 31, 2023 article, written on the *Defense One* website about the lack of data, states, in part, as follows:

> "'There's no other data behind it. So understanding what that is off of that one video is unlikely to occur—whereas today we have a lot of data where somebody sees something, there's gonna be a lot more data associated with it that we can pull out, radar data, and optical data, and [infrared] data.'
>
> That's one reason the Department of Defense issued new guidance to services and combatant commands about retaining data.
>
> 'The way data is handled on these platforms is they don't they don't retain them at all, ever. I mean, they retain them for 24 hours usually if there was an incident on the platform, like there was a malfunction,' Kirkpatrick said."

However, testimony of *Nimitz* Carrier Group personnel demonstrates that all electronic data was removed immediately after the incident. Kirkpatrick's statement is contradicted by a percipient witness that personnel dressed in Air Force uniforms removed all electronic data of the "tic-tac" incidents immediately thereafter.[37] Either that data was removed to preserve data about the incidents or to destroy the data. AARO should be trying to determine whether the data is still held by the Air Force or by personnel masquerading as Air Force officers. As discussed herein, similar episodes are common. Congress needs to learn about the

---

[36] https://www.defenseone.com/threats/2023/10/pentagon-may-never-get-bottom-famous-ufo-video/391672/.

[37] https://www.youtube.com/watch?v=Zmzc4YzDnN0.

electronic records taken from the *Nimitz* Carrier Group. This incident either can help establish the credibility of Commander Fravor or show there was a program to remove evidence of these incidents to prevent further study.

The contradiction between AARO Director Sean Kirkpatrick's statement steering interest anyway from one of the most documented incidents (U.S.S. *Nimitz*/tic-tac) on a probably faulty premise showed how AARO's approach has deviated from congressional intent. Even when there is evidence of anomalous behavior, the UAP program finds excuses to ignore it.

Soon after this Kirkpatrick statement, the DoD announced that the AARO Director was retiring in December 2023.[38] Even though AARO is only beginning its implementation of UAP law, Kirkpatrick is stepping down "after achieving his goals."[39] No successor was named, but Timothy A. Phillips was named Assistant Director and will serve in a dual role as assistant and acting director.

This rather surprising development follows a series of controversial missteps by Kirkpatrick that raised the ire of many in Congress. Congressional concern during 2022-2023 time period has included AARO decisions to prevent public disclosure of videos of UAP encounters; public criticism of a whistleblower who testified before Congress; two annual reports that failed to focus on the most serious cases; and the latest claim that there was no sensor data of the 2004 *Nimitz* "tic-tac" incidents. Despite personnel claiming the sensor data was removed by Air Force officers, Kirkpatrick stated that the 2004 sensor data was destroyed immediately after the

---

[38]https://www.defense.gov/News/Releases/Release/Article/3583248/statement-by-deputy-secretary-of-defense-kathleen-hicks-on-the-upcoming-departu/.

[39] https://metro.co.uk/2023/11/09/pentagon-ufo-boss-steps-down-after-explosive-admission-19798857/; https://thedebrief.org/pentagon-confirms-retirement-of-aaro-director-sean-kirkpatrick-as-new-deputy-director-is-named/.

incidents. Despite these missteps, Deputy Secretary of Defense Kathleen Hicks stated:

> "His (Kirkpatrick) commitment to transparency with the United States Congress and the American public on UAP leaves a legacy the department will carry forward as AARO continues its mission."

The AARO record does not support this statement. Only one video (metallic orb), recorded somewhere in the Middle East, is the only UAP video ever released to the public by AARO. A follow up interview of Kirkpatrick indicated that there were many more similar sensor videos showing the same type of unknown object.[40]

Kirkpatrick's LinkedIn post about whistleblower Grusch's congressional testimony was perhaps his biggest misstep. Criticism, as a private citizen, of Grusch's July 2023 testimony gave his superiors the right to terminate him for this outburst because it limited his ability to work with Congress.

For public employees, the right to speak freely as a private citizen is limited to speech that does not impact their ability to perform their job. Legal precedent holds that public officials may be terminated for speaking out in a way that impacts the official's job. His ability to liaison with Congress was harmed by his own personal comments.[41]

Whether Kirkpatrick's retirement was a product of any of this problematic behavior, it leaves AARO without permanent leadership at a time when congressional confidence in the Pentagon UAP program is waning and multiple deadlines are approaching. The result of his retirement without a new director being ready for appointment will delay the work of AARO. It leaves AARO with a

---

[40] https://thehill.com/opinion/national-security/4301944-aliens-or-a-foreign-power-pentagon-ufo-chief-says-someone-is-in-our-backyard/.

[41] Garcetti v. Ceballos, 547 U.S. 410 (2006).

new deputy director who will have to fill two jobs at once while learning on the job.[42]

The timing of these personnel moves, whether intentional or not, serves the historic pattern of delay in seeking answers to the UAP dilemma. Recent statements by outgoing Director Kirkpatrick may also indicate a new DoD/ODNI strategy. Coupled with recent statements from Kirkpatrick about a draft academic paper he co-authored with Harvard professor Avi Loeb, the specter of a change in DoD policy towards UAP may be in the offing.[43]

In the draft academic paper, Kirkpatrick and Professor Loeb consider whether some UAP may be probes sent from unmanned missions launched by civilizations in nearby solar systems. Loeb believes that the interstellar object, Oumuamua, may have been a sub-light speed spacecraft. Unmanned craft could be launching small probes towards Earth and that could explain the metallic orbs like the ones in the video released during congressional testimony in 2023 by Kirkpatrick and the 2017 GOFAST video. In the 2023 annual report released by ODNI, 25% of UAP are orbs.[44]

While this interstellar possibility accounts for some, but not all, reports, it could give the DoD a fall back argument to account for unexplained UAP. Painting these probes as drone-like objects that were sent to Earth by slow moving unoccupied craft can solve several headaches for DoD/ODNI. It would answer the question about the presence of technology beyond our grasp without the

---

[42] https://thedebrief.org/pentagon-confirms-retirement-of-aaro-director-sean-kirkpatrick-as-new-deputy-director-is-named/.

[43] https://lweb.cfa.harvard.edu/~loeb/LK1.pdf; https://www.msn.com/en-us/news/us/ufo-head-steps-down-after-acknowledging-evidence-of-activity-being-investigated-by-u-s-government/ar-AA1jJcbn.

[44] https://www.dni.gov/index.php/newsroom/reports-publications/reports-publications-2023/3733-2023-consolidated-annual-report-on-unidentified-anomalous-phenomena.

worrying problem of non-terrestrial biological entities visiting our planet. Small, non-threatening objects sent by unoccupied vehicles that took possibly thousands of years to arrive in our solar system would show that there is other life in the universe. It would do so in a way that demonstrates there is no potential threat of a non-terrestrial presence on Earth. Essentially, an ET-lite version of the UAP mystery shown in the GOFAST video. This hypothesis would ignore the 40-foot "tic-tac" seen in the FLIR video and the Gimble video taken by U.S.S. *Theodore Roosevelt* flight personnel. This scenario could form a "fire wall" for DoD/ODNI that stops further inquiry into more potentially disturbing encounters witnessed by military pilots. Only time will tell whether this ET-lite theory will become a fallback Pentagon policy.

Overall, using declassified records and testimony from public officials, the bulk of this book reviews similar moments in the government's UFO/UAP history. The early days of government UFO policy formation appear to start at the highest level of government. Presidents and their closest advisors were involved. Over time and as presidential administrations came and went, control of UAP issues appears to have retreated farther away into a shadowy world, away from the prying eyes of congressional oversight. Even many high-ranking military officials seem unaware of the seriousness of the issue. During the post-WWII era, it was a time of citizen trust in government. This trust was misplaced when it came to flying saucers. Other events in the world, such as the startling rise of communism after World War II, also appear to have influenced the government's early approach to UAP. While the unclassified historical information currently available to the public does not provide definitive answers, it helps us start to understand why we are in this current state of affairs. One where elected officials are unaware of what has been happening behind the scenes for the last 80 years.

CHAPTER THREE

THE FLYING SAUCER "PROBLEM"

The work product in the 2021 *Preliminary Assessment* was impeded by the non-cooperation of two key players, the Air Force and CIA. With the focus of the UAP inquiry on the possibility that UAP constitute a threat, two important sources of relevant information declined to meaningfully cooperate with the Navy's UAP Task Force. The *Preliminary Assessment* and the 2023 annual report both documented the failure of the CIA to cooperate at all. The CIA and its world-wide foreign intelligence apparatus could not be bothered to communicate with either UAPTF or AARO, even though congressional concern is whether one of our terrestrial adversaries is the source of this worrying phenomenon.

The Air Force, the military branch tasked with studying UFOs for decades, took a similar approach. In November 2020, the Air Force began a six-month "pilot" sighting report program. This program ended in March 2021, when the *Preliminary Assessment* was being finalized. This pilot program contributed little to the *Preliminary Assessment*, with most of the report's data coming from naval aviators. Yet, looking back at history, their reluctance to participate is understandable. CIA and Air Force reticence can be traced to the beginning of the "flying saucer era." Both followed their longstanding policies of denial about the phenomenon rather than help the ODNI and Secretary of Defense respond to a legitimate congressional inquiry. To understand this behavior, one must look to the past.

During the summer of 1947, a flying saucer wave swept the nation. Private pilot Kenneth Arnold, while searching for a plane crash in eastern Washington, saw nine objects that skipped through the air like a "saucer on water." While other sightings pre- dated Arnold's, his captured the nation's imagination. Within days of Mr. Arnold's report, other sighting reports started coming in. From July 4–9, 1947, discs were sighted in Washington, Oregon, Idaho, and California by pilots including two commercial, two Air Force, and one aviation magazine editor.[45] However, most of the reports came from untrained observers.

The United States government, the scientific community, and the national media got off to a rocky start explaining the possible presence of superior technology in our skies.[46] There was no uniform policy for dealing with the effects of the phenomenon. The same questions were asked as those recently asked by members of Congress. Did the phenomenon pose a genuine threat to national security? If so, who was behind the threat? Had the Russians made a giant technological leap? Were we testing secret weapons? As today, answers were not forthcoming from the military or intelligence community.

The newly formed Air Force had difficulty coping with the phenomenon. They assigned responsibility to the Air Technical Intelligence Center (ATIC) at Wright-Patterson Air Force Base (Wright Field until 1948) in Dayton, Ohio. Case investigations were handled by a small staff. Most reports were taken by local Air Force base intelligence officers and sent to ATIC where case determinations were made. 1947 saw a flood of reports, but most had prosaic explanations. From mid-1947 through early 1949, the

---

[45] National Investigations Committee on Aerial Phenomenon (NICAP), Richard H. Hall (Editor), *The UFO Evidence* (1964), reprint Barnes & Noble Books (1997), p. 33.

[46] Ruppelt, E., *The Report on Unidentified Flying Objects*, readaclassic.com (2010), reprint of 1956 original version, pp. 31, 62–63, 67, 85–88.

ATIC personnel eventually broke into two camps. Those in favor of considering an extraterrestrial hypothesis and those against.

Just like today, other explanations were considered and discarded. The Air Force denied that flying saucers were a secret military program. They also discarded the idea that the phenomenon was of foreign terrestrial origin. Why would a foreign power test a new weapon over the United States? The risk of loss and the possibility that the technology would fall into the wrong hands was too great. Swedish "ghost rockets," World War II "foo fighters," and New Mexico "green fireballs" added to the confusion.

Two significant incidents kept the phenomenon from disappearing from the public eye even as the number of post-1947 sightings dwindled. On January 7, 1948, a plane crash occurred in Kentucky that changed many people's perspective about the phenomenon.[47] Fort Knox's Godman Field received a UFO report from the Kentucky Highway Patrol. It was also reported that a 300-foot-wide UFO was flying near the base. An incoming flight of P-51 fighter planes (high performance, propeller aircraft) were asked to investigate. The lead pilot, Captain Thomas Mantell, chased what he called, according to a disputed account from the air traffic controllers, "an object of tremendous size." Having left the rest of his wing behind, Capt. Mantell chased the object to an altitude of 20,000 feet. An experienced combat pilot, Mantell did so without oxygen, beyond recommended altitudes. While chasing the object, his plane crashed, killing him, and leaving a mystery behind.

The Air Force first claimed he was chasing Venus in broad daylight. However, Venus was barely visible and would only be a pinprick of light that the observer would have to know where to look to even find. An alternative explanation was he was chasing a weather balloon. However, at the time, no balloon was in the area.

---

[47] Ibid, @ pp. 190, 211–215; Clark, Jerome, *The UFO Book: Encyclopedia of the Extraterrestrial* (1998), Visible Ink Press, pp. 351–356.

The Air Force went back and forth with various explanations, but none matched the facts. This was the first publicly acknowledged fatality involving a flying saucer. It added a worrisome element to the debate about the origin of flying saucers.

While post-1947 sightings declined, the quality of sightings improved.[48] A higher percentage of the 1948 and 1949 sightings were by credible observers. Pilots, law enforcement, scientists, and other trained observers were giving detailed accounts that could not be easily dismissed as "mass hysteria" or "war nerves."[49] The quality of the observer added to the Air Force's dilemma in trying to tamp down public concern. People trained in observational skills were speaking to the press about their sightings.

Another example was a sighting by airline pilots that raised air safety questions. On July 24, 1948, an Eastern Airlines flight was flying near Montgomery, Alabama. Pilot Clarence Chiles and Copilot Charles Whitted were at an altitude of 5,000 feet, preparing to land. An unknown object appeared in the distance. As it got closer, they noticed that it was shaped like the fuselage of a passenger plane without wings or a tail. The craft had two rows of windows and the bottom glowed blue. It had orangish flames appearing to come out of the back. The object came within a half a mile while they were on landing approach in restricted airspace. The pilots estimated that the object was about 500 feet higher than their position when it streaked past the DC-6, four-engine aircraft. While most passengers were asleep at the time, one passenger, a respected business executive, saw a blue streak go by the plane, confirming the pilots' description.[50] The sighting made national

---

[48] Ruppelt, E., *The Report on Unidentified Flying Objects*, readaclassic.com (2010), reprint of 1956 original version, pp. 109, 219, 223.

[49] Ibid, @ pp. 5, 64, 225.

[50] Clark, Jerome, *The UFO Book: Encyclopedia of the Extraterrestrial*, Visible Ink Press (1998), pp. 33–35.

news. The Chiles/Whitted sighting was unique in that they had a remarkably close-up look at the object. It was not just "lights in the sky."

As with the Mantell incident, air safety issues were raised. The DC-6 was on landing approach when the unknown object made a high speed pass in restricted airspace. The sighting came at a time when the Air Force was trying to reassure the public that the phenomenon was not a threat. The incident fanned public interest at a time when sightings were on the wane. It seemed that, just when the Air Force thought it was over the hump, the phenomenon would reappear and raise new concerns.

Air Force Captain Edward J. Ruppelt, Senior Officer for the Air Force's Project Blue Book, commented that the Mantell crash, and the Chiles/Whitted sighting created quite a stir among the Project Sign personnel. Sign was a predecessor program to Project Blue Book. Both incidents breathed new life into the extraterrestrial hypothesis. According to ATIC personnel, Captain Ruppelt and Major Dewey J. Fournet, Jr., an *Estimate of the Situation* was prepared by ATIC, including discussion of the possibility of extraterrestrial visitation. The *Estimate* was sent up the chain of command. When it reached Air Force Chief of Staff Hoyt S. Vandenberg, he rejected its conclusions and ordered all copies destroyed.[51]

The rejection of this memorandum indicated to ATIC that senior brass discouraged any discussion of the extraterrestrial hypothesis. It was considered a turning point. While there were many high-quality unexplained sightings at the time, the official Air Force policy no longer considered extraterrestrial visitation as a possible option. The DoD has not changed that assessment to this day.

---

[51] Ibid, @ pp. 177–179.

The Air Force ended one investigation program (Project Sign) and began another program with different priorities. As the new Project Grudge began in February 1949, the Air Force study began to live up to the new project designation, Grudge. However, the program's public title was Project Saucer, a less confrontational designation.

Project Grudge implemented the new emphasis, reflecting General Vandenberg's order to not consider any extraterrestrial hypothesis. This policy change is reflected in the final report of Project Sign, issued as Project Grudge began. This report lays out some of the early assumptions made by the Air Force's public face of its investigation of the phenomenon. Psychological aspects were front and center as a reason for many sightings. The report suggests that more analysis is necessary relating to psychological causes of sightings. This conclusion foretells the joint CIA/Air Force approach to the phenomenon.

Another issue raised by the Project Sign final report was the early involvement of the FBI in the UFO phenomenon. The FBI assisted Project Sign investigation of witness reliability. Despite the repeated claims by the FBI of non-involvement since September 1947, this public report specifically calls out the assistance of the FBI under its counter-intelligence authority. On this point, the report states, in part, as follows:

> "The Federal Bureau of Investigation has assisted Project 'Sign' in a number of instances, both by investigations of character and reliability of witnesses and by providing other investigative services."[52]

Since there were no law enforcement reasons behind this "assistance," the authority for these investigations must be justified

---

[52] https://archive.org/details/ProjectSIGN/mode/2up. *Unidentified Aerial Objects: Project Sign*, technical report no. F-TR-2274-IA, @ p. 3 (12 of 72).

under the FBI's counterintelligence authority. The Air Force used FBI personnel to investigate a mystery officially determined not to be a national security threat. Until the present, the FBI still claims it was not involved in UAP study. Use of the federal government's counterintelligence arm belies claims of no defense interest in the mystery. It also foreshadows the establishment of a "debunking" program where the main priority was to denigrate UFO witnesses with the aim to depress interest in the subject.

As a guidepost that points to the beginnings of a stage-managed approach to the subject, the Project Sign final report further explains the reasoning behind the Air Force refusal to consider a non-terrestrial source of these mysterious objects. The change in Air Force approach helped to allay public distress while 1948-1949 sightings actually should have raised more national security concerns. Despite the current lack of answers, the Air Force still refuses to admit consideration of a non-terrestrial source of UAP. On this point, the Project Sign final report states as follows:

> "Another possibility is that these aerial objects are visitors from another planet.... Pending elimination of all other solutions or definite proof of the nature of these objects, this policy will not be explored."[53]

To this day, the DoD has held fast to this position. The 1949 public report confirmed the "no possibility of an ET source" study limitation, setting the direction of its chief of staff, Hoyt Vandeberg. There could be no consideration of a non-terrestrial cause of flying saucers.

At the time, many sensitive military facilities were in the State of New Mexico. New Mexico experienced many sightings around White Sands military area and other sensitive bases. Near the end of 1948, a phenomenon called "green fireballs" occurred almost

---

[53] Ibid, @ p. 9 (18 of 72).

exclusively over New Mexico airspace. While the Air Force's public position was predominantly dismissive of the phenomenon, some Air Force elements were still concerned. In 1952, Captain Ruppelt transitioned from studying Soviet MIG jet aircraft wreckage to a new program, Project Blue Book. He began work on organizing flying saucer reports from 1947 onward. He documented the decrease in sightings during 1948–1951, while reporting that the quality of sightings was improving. As time went on, the public began to pay less attention to sightings. However, in 1952, the number of sightings increased dramatically. The summer of 1952 saw some of the most disturbing sightings to date. According to Ruppelt, the 158 leading newspapers in the country published approximately 16,000 items about flying saucers during just a six-month period in 1952.[54] Even restricted airspace over Washington, D.C. became a target of the phenomenon.[55] Over a two-week period in late July 1952, Washington, D.C. had many visual sightings that were confirmed on radar. At least one radar-confirmed sighting was over the White House.

The phenomenon reasserted itself as flying saucers returned to the front pages of the nation's newspapers. A "wave" of sightings caused the narrative that flying saucers were "not a threat" to lose its public appeal. Information about the saucers once again became a hot ticket, and the media provided the public what it wanted.[56] In

---

[54] Ruppelt, Edward J.: *The Report on Unidentified Flying Objects* (Original 1956 Edition) Doubleday & Company (1956), reissued Cosimo Classics (2011). Before the Internet and 24-hour cable news, an important research tool used by the Air Force was newspaper clipping services. They would supply the subscriber with stories from national and local newspapers about any topic. They did not cover every newspaper, but a substantial portion of the nation's newspapers. This helped the Air Force keep up with sighting reports.

[55] Clark, Jerome, *The UFO Book: Encyclopedia of the Extraterrestrial*, Visible Ink Press (1998), pp. 653–662.

[56] For instance, *True Magazine* sold more copies of its January 1950 Edition with a flying saucer article than any other edition. *True* was a men's

order to address concerns over the Washington, D.C. sightings, the Pentagon held its largest post-World War II press conference. Multiple visual sightings with radar confirmations changed the public's perspective, and the military was subject to scrutiny over its "no threat" conclusions. Testimony of Civil Aeronautics Authority[57] personnel were that the radar returns showed real objects that could make right angle turns at incredible speeds. The testimony was that the radar blips were too strong and could not be attributed to false readings caused by temperature inversions or ground returns. The press was no longer assuming that the government explanations of false radar readings were accurate. The resurgence of the phenomenon placed both the Air Force and the CIA with a dilemma of how to address a problem that they thought had been successfully handled until the summer of 1952.

---

magazine that focused on tales of hunting, fishing, and other "manly" experiences. (http://www.project1947.com/fig/truejan1950.htm.)

[57] The CAA was the forerunner to the Federal Aviation Administration (FAA). The CAA employed the air traffic controllers that, along with military personnel at Andrews Air Force base, monitored the phenomenon on radar. Many of the radar sightings were later recanted by air traffic controllers after they were interviewed by military officials.

CHAPTER FOUR

THE "PROBLEM" IS DEFINED

The Washington, D.C. sightings sparked nationwide interest. The Truman Administration needed to respond. Even the President publicly speculated about the mystery. The White House asked for the CIA to become involved and make recommendations about the latest surge in sightings. Many declassified documents from this era simply describe the UFO issue as the "problem."[58] As the CIA was brought into the mix, it quickly established a working relationship with the Air Force. Now, the worry was about the probability of new sightings by quality witnesses in the summer of 1953. To regain the narrative, the Air Force and CIA would have to reduce the number of quality sightings known to the public.

Any review of the flying saucer era must consider the origins and makeup of the two arms of the federal government given responsibility over the UFO "problem." In 1947, the flying saucer problem was assigned to the newly created Air Force, followed by Central Intelligence Agency (CIA) involvement, as reports surged. Both the Air Force and the CIA were created in order to help the U.S. face the new challenges of the Cold War. Congress passed the National Security Act (Public Law 80-253 (effective July 26, 1947)), which established the Air Force as a separate branch of the military. The law also created the CIA. These two organizations set in

---

[58] *i.e.*, "Flying Saucers Problem," October 14, 1952, https://www.cia.gov/readingroom/docs/CIA-RDP81R00560R000100020010-9.pdf.

motion the policies that determined how the phenomenon and people associated with it were treated.

The CIA became the main intelligence-gathering body within the executive branch, filling a gap left after the World War II Office of Strategic Services (OSS) was disbanded. The restructuring of the military and the creation of enhanced intelligence gathering became a national priority with bipartisan support. The public, with its understandable fears of communism in the emerging nuclear era, placed its faith in the military and the newly created intelligence community to address these threats. Despite a pathetic early record of accomplishment, the CIA was held in high esteem and barely questioned by elected officials.[59] When the CIA was formed, Congress did not establish direct oversight. Congress had no dedicated intelligence oversight committees until the 1970s.

The emergence of a possible extraterrestrial threat could not have come at a worse time. In addition to the rapid expansion of communism and with European allies still recovering from the most destructive war in human history, this new threat posed challenges beyond comprehension. In 1947, changes to the national security and military structure played a large role in how these challenges were faced. From the rise of communism to the flying saucer problem, the military/intelligence challenges were met by newly created organizations. Undefined boundaries of bureaucratic responsibilities were still present when a CIA scientific panel was formed in January 1953 to look into the "problem."

Section 102 of the National Security Act established the Central Intelligence Agency. Its mission was to create an apparatus to provide intelligence about the threats to the United States from

---

[59] Talbot, David, *The Devil's Chessboard: Allen Dulles, the CIA, and the Rise of America's Secret Government*, HarperCollins (2015), p. 249. In October 1954, Gen. James Doolittle (ret.) explained to President Eisenhower in an Oval Office meeting that the CIA was badly managed and had no congressional oversight.

foreign sources. The CIA was statutorily prohibited from having "police, subpoena, law-enforcement powers or internal-security functions." This prohibition left the FBI in charge of counterespionage authority within the boundaries of the U.S. As we will see, this restriction was not taken seriously by the CIA when UFOs were involved.

This prohibition was intended to keep the CIA out of domestic matters in contrast to the KGB (Committee for State Security) and its surveillance program of Soviet citizens. This law became known as the CIA's "no domestic spying" prohibition. The FBI and CIA were required to coordinate the FBI's domestic law enforcement with the external threat responsibilities of the CIA. (61 U.S. Stats. §102(e).)

Generally, the CIA was able to carry out policy largely outside of the public eye. Press coverage was based on information which rarely could be independently verified. This left no means to tell whether intelligence programs were working. By 1953, it started becoming apparent that its policies looked for short-term gains and gave lip service to democratic principles. Violating basic human rights was not a concern that got in the way of achieving intelligence community goals. Failures were routinely covered up and kept from Congress. These intelligence failures were typically not discovered until well after the fact. Funding was obtained with little or no congressional oversight. From the Eisenhower Administration's CIA Director Allen Dulles on down, many of the men in charge had an "ends justify the means" mentality that grew out of the Wild West attitude of the WWII OSS.[60]

---

[60] Talbot, David, *The Devil's Chessboard: Allen Dulles, the CIA, and the Rise of America's Secret Government*, HarperCollins (2015); Kinzer, Stephen, *The Brothers: John Foster Dulles, Allen Dulles, and Their Secret World War*, St. Martin Griffin (2014); Prados, John, *Safe For Democracy: The Secret Wars of the CIA*, Ivan R. Dee (2006).

It wasn't until the 1970s, with the Senate intelligence oversight review (known as the "Church Committee" after its Chair, Senator Frank Church (D-ID)) that many of the intelligence excesses of the 1950s were revealed. By this time, many of the failures, such as Guatemala, Iran, MK-Ultra (LSD/mind control experiments on U.S. citizens) and others, had done long-term damage to U.S. interests.[61]

It is within this backdrop that the CIA scientific group known as the Robertson Panel worked. The Robertson Panel operated in secret, with no congressional authorization. Its recommendations were selectively circulated throughout the executive branch's diplomatic, military and intelligence agencies. However, its recommendations were not shared with Congress. As discussed, this new intelligence apparatus was faced with a challenging world. The "ends justified the means" approach to military/intelligence issues colored the way the UFO phenomenon was handled.

---

[61] Ibid, Church Committee (U.S. Senate Select Committee on Intelligence Activities Within the United States), *Intelligence Activities and the Rights of Americans: 1976 U.S. Senate Report on Illegal Wiretaps and Domestic Spying by the FBI, CIA and NSA*, Red and Black Publishers (2007).

CHAPTER FIVE

THE COLD WAR BACKDROP

The role the United States played on the world stage was still in flux with the start of the flying saucer era. The Truman Administration was forced to juggle two potential threats. The rapid world-wide expansion of communism and the mysterious flying saucer phenomenon. One concern was front and center, while the other was seen on the surface to most as a pop culture phenomenon. By 1953, Presidential administrations changed from the Democratic Party to Republican, in large part, in reaction to the spread of communism. While the Republican Party had been primarily isolationist prior to World War II, its post-war foreign policy outlook took a more proactive, hard-line approach to the country's new global responsibilities.

At the time, the United States was the preeminent world superpower, but still learning how to handle its new role. In the 1952 election cycle, Republicans claimed the Democrats were "soft on communism." In 1953, Republicans now controlled the House of Representatives, the Senate, and the White House. The Republican foreign policy was centered around its worldwide battle with communism and all military, intelligence, and foreign policy goals were structured to deal with this threat. Domestic policy reflected these fears, real or imagined.

Communism replaced fascism as the leading global threat to both democracy and free-market capitalism. All issues were seen through this prism. Its former ally, the Soviet Union, was consolidating its stranglehold on Eastern Europe. Italy, France, and Greece were flirting with communism as their democratically elected legislative bodies had substantial communist opposition parties. Washington, D.C. was deep into the Senator Joseph McCarthy (R-WI) led Red Scare. With little or no evidence, McCarthy claimed the State Department and the Army were riddled with Soviet spies.

Outside of Europe, the threats to U.S. leadership were multi-faceted. In Asia, the late 1940s saw the rise of communism in China, Viet Nam, and Korea. In China, Mao Zedong's Communist Party took control of mainland China and ousted Generalissimo Chiang Kai-shek, who fled to Formosa (Taiwan). The communists fought a guerilla war against the ruling party based mostly on class differences. It was a peasant revolution against feudal landlords and the government. As a result, the most populous country in the world became communist. "Who lost China" was a frequent topic in Washington, D.C. This meant that two of Washington's most populous WWII allies, China and the Soviet Union, were now enemies. Similar conflicts arose in Viet Nam and Korea.

After World War II, Viet Nam's monarchy collapsed, and the French tried to reestablish colonial rule. In 1954, the country was "temporarily" divided in two, with the northern portion ruled by agrarian communists. Viet Nam's divided governments were later to become a defining problem for the United States. However, in 1953, it was a French problem.

Korea, with help from the Soviet Union, established a communist government north of the 38th parallel. As part of an agreement between the Soviet Union and the United States, the Soviets withdrew their forces in 1948. The southern half was occupied by United States troops after World War II. The U.S. established a fledgling democracy in the South in 1948. The United States withdrew its troops in 1949. The north invaded the south on June 25, 1950, with the support of the Soviet Union. Soviet support was conditioned on Chinese troops if needed.

The United States sought United Nations approval for authority to repel the invasion. The Soviet Union had been boycotting the Security Council meetings in protest of Taiwan holding the Council's China seat. With the Soviet Union absent, the United States received approval from the Security Council on June 27, 1950, to support a defense of South Korea against invading armies from North Korea. It was the first approval of the use of force by the United Nations.

During the Truman Administration, U.S. military forces slowly gained the upper hand until massive numbers of Chinese troops joined the fight. After that point, neither side could claim victory, and a bloody stalemate settled over the Korean peninsula. The Eisenhower Administration continued peace talks started by the previous administration. On July 27, 1953, the U.S. signed an armistice ending hostilities in Korea. To date, no peace treaty has ever been signed. The Korean peninsula has lived with this uneasy armistice ever since.

In the 1950s, United States' relations with the Third World were guided by this communist-versus-free world/capitalism struggle. The Eisenhower Administration used clandestine methods to combat real and perceived communist threats. Non-aligned countries were expected to pick a side. Ones that strayed too close to the Soviet orbit were enticed and/or punished by the West.

Domestically, citizens who held socialist or communist views were ostracized. Citizens were scrutinized to see if they had any past socialist sympathies or support for the Soviet Union. Many unfairly fell under suspicion as being part of a movement to undermine American democracy. These leanings were generally tolerated during World War II, while the Soviet Union was our ally in the war against fascism. However, pro-Soviet views quickly came under suspicion with the rapid expansion of communism. The new Republican administration, backed by unwavering support from the majority Republican Congress, was free to take more aggressive actions in our worldwide struggle with communism.

It is against this backdrop that the Robertson Panel issued its report to new leadership at the CIA. Allen Dulles had moved up the ladder to become the Director of Central Intelligence. A former Office of Strategic Services (OSS) officer, Dulles was tolerated but not trusted by Truman. Allen Dulles was now working with his brother, John Foster Dulles, the new Secretary of State. When CIA matters came before Congress, the new mood was to give the CIA whatever it wanted to achieve its policy ends in this worldwide struggle. As a former OSS officer, Allen Dulles was no stranger to using nefarious means to achieve government policy. His main goals were to thwart communism and protect capitalism. This extended to his personal interests, which often mixed with his professional goals. Corporate clients of the Dulles brothers' former law firm, Sullivan & Cromwell, benefited from covert policies that mixed corporate and U.S. interests.[62]

Early in his tenure as Director of Central Intelligence (DCI), Dulles supported a coup in Iran, which deposed an elected government that opposed Western oil interests.[63] The ramifications of this interference are still being felt in our relations with Iran. In 1954, there was a CIA-backed coup in Guatemala that assisted a Sullivan & Cromwell client, United Fruit Company.[64] United Fruit had propped up a string of dictators and the coup had stopped a movement towards pro-democracy reforms. Since then, the country has continued to struggle. To this day, it is one of the poorest countries in Latin America. Poverty and crime are still reasons for asylum seekers coming to the U.S.

---

[62] Kinzer, Stephen, *The Brothers: John Foster Dulles, Allen Dulles, and Their Secret World War*, St. Martin Griffin (2014), pp. 101–103.

[63] Talbot, David, *The Devil's Chessboard: Allen Dulles, the CIA, and the Rise of America's Secret Government*, HarperCollins (2015), pp. 227–241.

[64] Ibid, @ pp. 251–266.

In April 1953, Dulles also gave the go ahead for the CIA's MK-Ultra program.[65] The program experimented on unwitting U.S. citizens to develop drugs used in interrogations. Participants were given drugs under false pretenses, resulting in many permanent disabilities and deaths. It was supervised by the CIA's Office of Scientific Intelligence (OSI) and assisted by the U.S. Army Biological Warfare Laboratory. As we will see, OSI was simultaneously responsible for handling the UFO "problem."

Similar disregard for the law can be seen with the implementation of Robertson Panel policies. This is hardly surprising when compared with other decisions made during the Dulles tenure. The OSI MK-Ultra program was one of many CIA excesses under the Dulles watch that were exposed in the mid-1970s by the U.S. Senate's Church Committee chaired by Idaho Senator Frank Church (D-ID). The Robertson Panel and the MK-Ultra program were not subject to any congressional oversight during the 1950s.[66] This lack of oversight reflected a protect-America-by-any-means approach.

It was against this backdrop that the federal government addressed the flying saucer "problem." Institutions were reorganized to deal with the existential threat of communism. For the first time in human history, armed conflict could result in the destruction of life on this planet. The stakes had never been higher. In a world mostly exhausted by war, new challenges were adding up. Rebuilding Europe, stemming the tide of communism, and navigating a world going through the end of European colonialism

---

[65] Kinzer, Stephen, *The Brothers: John Foster Dulles, Allen Dulles, and Their Secret World War,* St. Martin Griffin (2014), p. 115.

[66] Church Committee (U.S. Senate Select Committee on Intelligence Activities Within the United States), *Intelligence Activities and the Rights of Americans: 1976 U.S. Senate Report on Illegal Wiretaps and Domestic Spying by the FBI, CIA and NSA,* Red and Black Publishers (2007).

were among the multifaceted challenges faced. Add to these challenges a phenomenon that was both perplexing and potentially the most threatening of all.

CHAPTER SIX

THE CIA TACKLES THE "PROBLEM"

After the 1947 flying saucer wave, sightings dwindled in the United States. This changed in 1952. According to Project Bluebook, in July 1952, there were 250 reports nationwide, with a 28% "unidentified" rate.[67] For a two-week period some refer to as the "Washington flap," Washington, D.C. had numerous visual sightings that were confirmed on radar.[68] While explanations for the sightings changed to "conventional" causes, the government explanations were contradicted by the weight of the evidence.

During the Washington flap, the military sent planes after radar blips.[69] Each time fighter planes were vectored to the location of the radar targets; the objects would leave. After the fighter jets returned to base, the UFOs would return. Radar personnel at Washington National Airport could see some of the UFOs by standing outside the tower, seeing them in locations that matched radar. Others throughout the region corroborated the visual sightings.

Official explanations were of weather inversions and lights reflecting off clouds. These explanations were contradicted by trained eyewitnesses, although there were abrupt changes in testimony after air traffic control witnesses were interviewed by federal agents. Professionals with technical knowledge of radar

---

[67] Flying saucers, October 2, 1952, DOC 0005515933.

[68] Clark, Jerome, *The UFO Book: Encyclopedia of the Extraterrestrial*, Visible Ink Press (1998), pp. 351–356.

[69] https://www.ufointernationalproject.com/ufo-photos-and-videos/washington-dc-film-footage-1952/.

dismissed the weather inversion and light reflection explanations as highly improbable considering the conditions that existed at the time. Regardless of who was correct, the public was concerned. Our advanced fighter jets could only temporarily chase them away. In 1952, UFOs were also spotted at sensitive military installations around the country. While the objects did not take any aggressive actions, much of the public was understandably concerned and looked to the military to reassure them. In the immediate aftermath of the Washington flap, Air Force Intelligence's General John Alexander Samford held the largest post-World War II military press conference to reassure a nervous public that the government had the situation under control.[70] Meanwhile, President Truman openly wondered about the phenomenon. He ordered the CIA to investigate the matter.

Soon after the Washington, D.C. sightings, CIA personnel significantly increased involvement in the study of "unidentified aerial objects." Within days, H. Marshall Chadwell (Assistant Director of Scientific Intelligence) wrote a memo to the Deputy Director/Intelligence that recommended a special study group be formed and a report issued regarding recent developments by August 15th.[71] The August 1, 1952, CIA internal memo stated, in part, as follows:

> "2. Notwithstanding the foregoing tentative facts, so long as a series of reports remains 'unexplainable' (interplanetary aspects and alien origin not being thoroughly excluded from consideration) caution requires that intelligence continue coverage of the subject.

---

[70] https://www.youtube.com/watch?v=bAGZQT8FSPk.

[71] "Recent Sightings of Unexplained Objects (July 29, 1952)," http://www.nicap.org/docs/wns/wns3.htm.

3. It is recommended that **CIA surveillance of subject matter**, in coordination with proper authorities of primary operational concern at ATIC (Air Force), **be continued.** It is strongly urged, however, that no indication of CIA interest or concern reach the press or public, in view of their probable alarmist tendencies to accept such interest as 'confirmatory' of the soundness of 'unpublished facts' in the hands of the U.S. government."[72] (*emphasis added.*)

A "comprehensive briefing" was scheduled by the CIA Special Study Group on August 8, 1952. After the briefing, the CIA's Physics & Electronics Division was tasked "to take a stand and to formulate an opinion as might be required" to deal with flying saucers.[73]

On August 19th, the CIA held a briefing on the status of Agency efforts to date. A partial transcript indicates what the CIA Study Group had gleaned from its Air Force August 8 meeting and other efforts. While there was dissent, the predominant view was that, given enough evidence, the "unknowns" could be reduced to zero. The focus of these early consultations wasn't just about the UFO phenomenon itself. Without evidence, the Air Force stated that it believed some UFO groups contained elements with questionable loyalty. Finally, the Air Force's main concern was the use of flying saucer sightings as a mask for a Soviet air invasion. Each of these elements would later form the basis of the CIA's position on the matter.[74]

---

[72] "Flying saucers," August 1, 1952, CIA-RDP81R00560R000100020015-4.

[73] "Minutes of Branch Chief's Meeting," (August 11, 1952), DOC 0000015441.pdf.

[74] Partial Transcript of CIA Briefing (August 19, 1952), http://cufon.org/cufon/cia-52-1.htm.

On September 11, 1952, a memo, entitled "Flying Saucers," was forwarded to Director of Central Intelligence (DCI) Walter Bedell Smith by H. Marshall Chadwell, Assistant Director of the Office of Scientific Intelligence (OSI). It was likely prepared by Deputy Assistant Director Philip Strong, asking the following:

> "To determine:
>
> a.   Whether there are national security implications in the problem of 'unidentified flying objects' i.e. flying saucers.
>
> b.   Whether adequate study and research is currently being directed to this problem in its relation to such national security implications; and
>
> c.   What further investigation and research should be instituted, by whom and under what aegis."[75]

The assignment was approved by Truman's CIA Director Smith and identifies the "problem"; its "national security" implications; and, if further research is necessary, who gets the assignment? CIA OSI recommended that a study group be formed to:

> "1. Analyze and systematize the factors of information which form the fundamental problem.
>
> 2. Determine the fields of fundamental science which must be investigated in order to reach an understanding of the phenomenon involved; and
>
> 3. Make recommendations for the initiation of appropriate research."[76]

---

[75] "Flying saucers" (September 11, 1952), DOC 0000015343.pdf.

[76] Ibid.

A CIA consultant panel recommended the formation of a study group to do a science-based analysis of the "problem." This recommendation stated that the "solutions would probably be found on the margins or just beyond the frontiers of our present knowledge in the fields of atmospheric, ionospheric, and extraterrestrial phenomenon...." The memo mentions that the Massachusetts Institute of Technology (MIT) had indicated an interest in forming such a group. MIT would have been a logical choice. It was already hosting Project Lincoln, which was an Air Force sponsored air defense project. At the time, MIT had a longstanding relationship with the military. During and after World War II, MIT's Dr. Vannevar Bush oversaw scientific projects that developed weapons for the military. He was the country's leading voice on the application of science to solve military problems. He counseled both Presidents Roosevelt and Truman on the scientific applications to military projects.[77] These connections made MIT a logical choice to do any needed scientific research.

The final recommendation in the September 11 memo did not accept the in-depth scientific study option of its consultant group. It narrowed the research question to quick identification of the phenomenon. The recommendation did not include research of the phenomenon's source or purpose. H. Marshall Chadwell recommended to DCI Walter Bedell Smith that the White House's National Security Council be advised of the security implications of flying saucers. The "security implications" were limited in scope to "empower" the Director of Central Intelligence to consult with other agencies, either inside or outside of government, to "solve the problem of instant positive identification of 'unidentified flying objects.'" Second, it was recommended to the DCI and the White House National Security Council that the CIA be assigned

---

[77] According to a declassified Canadian document from this period, Dr. Bush had been appointed to lead a highly classified effort to study UFOs (http://www.majesticdocuments.com/pdf/smithmemo-21nov51.pdf).

authority to develop offensive and defensive uses of the phenomenon. Finally, once this research was ready, the CIA would recommend to the National Security Council "a policy of public information which will minimize the risk of panic."

The three policy recommendations do not include any scientific effort to determine the nature of the phenomenon. The MIT scientific study proposal, which would have been an extension of the work it was already doing for the Air Force, was rejected. The MIT recommendation would have addressed broader questions about the phenomenon besides its short-term, Cold War defense implications.

Considering this one memo in isolation, how these recommendations are framed may not indicate a predisposition about the phenomenon. However, as will be discussed, the recommended course of action was framed with the intent to limit inquiry to establishing whether a threat exists in relation to the Soviet Union. The study would not focus on whether flying saucers exist as a physical reality. Rather than study the nature of the phenomenon, the charge was to first see how we could defend against use of the phenomenon by the Soviets to mask an aerial attack. Second, could it be exploited for psychological warfare purposes at home and against our enemies? The broader and possibly more serious long-term threat of unknown origin was ignored.

By October 2, 1952, the preliminary inquiry was finished, and a memorandum was sent by H. Marshall Chadwell to CIA Director Walter Bedell Smith.[78] This memo had an attachment dated September 24, 1952, which provided more detail about the 13-day investigation of the Office of Scientific Intelligence, likely its Physics & Electronics Division. During this investigation period, a team from the CIA's OSI consulted with the Air Force Special

---

[78] "Flying saucers," October 2, 1952, DOC 0005515933.

Studies Group at the Air Technical Intelligence Center (ATIC), Wright-Patterson Air Force Base. This Air Force group oversaw investigations of flying saucer sightings. The Air Force representatives shared sighting data showing a much higher rate of sightings in the first half of 1952, with July having 250 official sighting reports alone.[79]

Despite a higher percentage of 1952 unexplained sightings, the memo limits its recommendations for the DCI to ancillary effects of the phenomenon. The memo first discusses the psychological implications of the phenomenon and whether it can be (1) controlled, (2) predicted or (3) used for psychological warfare, either offensively or defensively. The second aspect of the phenomenon that was recommended for study was whether it caused an "air vulnerability" and might interfere with threat identification in case of a sneak attack by the Soviet Union. The memo also recommends two referrals, one to the National Security Council (NSC) at the White House and another to the CIA's Psychological Strategy Review Board. While the language of these referrals was attached to the October 2nd memo, neither attachment has been declassified. Because the memo to the Psychological Strategy Review Board is still classified, we do not know if it made recommendations for the Board to look at domestic uses of the phenomenon.

Once again, both reasons given for further study did not relate to the nature of the phenomenon itself. Further study by the CIA was recommended to either minimize the risk of a surprise attack by the USSR or to gain a tactical advantage over the Soviet Union in case of a war. From an operational perspective, one of the reasons to study the problem was stated as follows:

---

[79] Ibid.

"8.(c) In order to minimize risk of panic, a rational policy should be established as to what should be told to the public regarding the phenomenon."[80]

Study of the "problem," in part, was to determine how to avoid psychological warfare impacts in case of a Soviet air invasion. The memo noted that there was no mention of the phenomenon in the Soviet press. Despite no mention of flying saucers in the Soviet-controlled media, the CIA wanted to figure out how to use flying saucers as an offensive weapon against the Soviets. How could the U.S. use flying saucers that few Soviet citizens had even heard about?

From declassified papers, it becomes apparent that CIA consideration of the "problem" was not aimed at finding out if it was real. The study's parameters were seen through the prism of U.S.-USSR conflict. At the time, the United States did not have complete radar coverage of possible Soviet bomber routes to the United States. Construction of radar installations for the Distant Early Warning Line (DEW Line) by the United States and Canada did not begin until December 1954. It became operational in 1957. This picket line of radar installations would detect a Soviet bomber attack coming from over the polar route. Until the DEW Line was constructed, defense forces relied, in small part, on civilian air defense personnel who made visual sightings and reported to the Air Force. The concern of a surprise attack was real, but reliance on the civilian population for early warning was never a serious option. Civilian plane spotters in the continental United States would provide little help. The "early warning" need was to detect Soviet aircraft over northern Canada or Alaska, not the continental United States. Domestically, the Federal Civil Defense Administration (FCDA) was focused on preparation for possible attacks, not their detection. Further, FCDA was never included in the policy

---

[80] Ibid.

formulation, but informed months after the policy was adopted by the Robertson Panel.[81] Any real concern about civil defense preparation in the continental U.S. would have to include FCDA.

Assuming they did not have any idea about the source of the phenomenon, one would think that the CIA would be interested in knowing the source and intentions of a phenomenon that, in the long run, could pose a greater threat than the Soviets. As shown in CIA reports, almost three in 10 sightings studied by the Air Force during the first seven months of 1952 were of "unknown" origin. This was the crucial period when the most sensitive airspace in the country was repeatedly violated. Yet, while the September 24, 1952 memo considered the subject of the highest importance, it was only recommending that the Director of Central Intelligence approve investigation related to "operational" issues of a potential Soviet air attack and psychological warfare.

Even with the limited scope of the study, the seriousness is reflected in the memo. Assistant Director H. Marshall Chadwell, in part, recommends:

> "I consider this problem to be of such importance that it should be brought to the attention of the National Security Council (White House), in order that a community-wide coordinated effort towards its solution may be initiated."[82]

The still-classified attachments to the October 2nd memorandum to the CIA Director were reports to the National Security Council and the CIA's Psychological Strategy Review Board. Based on the recommended actions, there seem to be two purposes. Preventing the Soviets from using UFO reports to help mask a sneak attack. Also, using the UFO phenomenon as a

---

[81] FCDA Meeting, April 23, 1953, DOC 0000015359.

[82] "Flying Saucers," September 24, 1952, p. 4, para. 11, DOC 0005515933.

psychological weapon, with the most likely target being the American people.

If the October 2nd memo is correct, there were no reports in Soviet media about flying saucers. We now know that Russia had sightings during this time of similar phenomenon. After the Cold War, much of this information became public. However, if there were no reports in the Soviet media at the time, it would be hard for the U.S. to use fake sightings as a psychological warfare tool. At this early stage of the Cold War, the CIA had few, if any, assets in the Soviet Union to launch a psychological warfare campaign.[83] The use of flying saucers as an offensive psychological weapon against the Soviets in 1952 was not a serious option. The other potential target was internal and a violation of CIA legal limitations against domestic security functions.

On October 20th or 21st, the CIA held a coordination meeting with the Defense Department. Invited personnel included General John A. Samford, Director of Intelligence for the Air Force. The General had held the Pentagon press conference after the July 1952 Washington, D.C. sightings. Dr. Walter G. Whitman, Chairman of the Defense Department's Research Development Board (RDB), was also an invitee. The RDB was a body of scientific and military personnel who directed defense-related scientific research.

> Prior to the meeting, there was an informal discussion held by the CIA's Deputy Director of Intelligence Loftus E. Becker, Director of Scientific Intelligence H. Marshall Chadwell, and Assistant Director Intelligence Coordination James Q. Reber. This informal group agreed that a program proposal be forwarded to the Director of Central Intelligence. The informal group wanted to develop a program quickly, rather than a lengthy study of the "problem"

---

[83] Kinzer, Stephen, *The Brothers: John Foster Dulles, Allen Dulles, and Their Secret World War,* St. Martin Griffin (2014), p. 155.

using "a great deal of formal, high-level paper pushing before taking action."[84]

The likelihood that any effort would lead to a better understanding of the phenomenon was set back by the move to recommend against a long-term scientific study. Even with no recommended long-term scientific study, CIA personnel still had discussions outside of the organization with academics and scientists about a possible scientific study. On December 2, 1952, Deputy Assistant Director Philip G. Strong, a key player on CIA UFO issues, met with Dr. Julius A. Stratton, Provost at MIT, and Dr. Max Millikan, Director of the MIT Center for International Studies, to discuss recent developments regarding UFOs. They discussed the possibility that MIT could study UFOs under its current Air Force study, Project Lincoln. They also discussed the possibility of other academic institutions being involved, namely Cal Tech and Princeton. Dr. Stratton asked to be informed on the progress of any analysis going forward, "being fully aware of the potential danger and implications of the situation."[85]

After meeting with the MIT executives, General Strong met with physicists Lloyd Berkner and Jerrold G. Zacharias to discuss the "problem." While Zacharias was not interested in the flying saucer problem, Berkner was highly interested. Berkner would later join the effort and write the Robertson Panel's report with CIA consultant and rocket expert Frederick Durant, Deputy Director for Scientific Intelligence Marshall Chadwell and, likely, Philip Strong.

The same day, December 2, 1952, H. Marshall Chadwell, issued a memo based on previous direction given by the Director of Central

---

[84] "Flying Saucers Problem," October 14, 1952, CIA-RDP81R00560R000100020010-9.pdf.

[85] Memorandum for the Record (Philip G. Strong, December 3, 1952), CIA-RDP81R00560R000100020007-3.

Intelligence, Walter Bedell Smith.[86] This memo had two attachments. The first was a memo from the DCI to the National Security Council and the second was a draft National Security Council directive prepared by the CIA. The cover memo raised concerns about UFOs, including stating:

"Sightings of unexplained objects at great altitudes and traveling at high speeds in the vicinity of major U.S. defense installations are of such nature that they are not attributable to natural phenomenon or known type of aerial vehicles."

This language was not in the two attachments sent to the White House NSC. The draft attachments warned of the need to direct various agencies' coordination to address the problem of instantly identifying UFOs. Identification of UFOs would prevent them from being confused with Soviet air vehicles and being used to create panic to mask a Soviet air attack. The directive from the NSC only addressed the "problem" as one of quick identification of UFOs to differentiate them from Soviet aerial military vehicles. The first directive gave the CIA authority as follows:

"The Director of Central Intelligence shall formulate and carry out a program of intelligence and research activities as required to solve the problem of instant positive identification of unidentified flying objects."[87]

The three other parts of the directive addressed coordination to avoid duplication. The information would be distributed as appropriate. While there is no declassified copy of a final version of a National Security Council directive, the declassified documents

---

[86] Memorandum to DCI re: Unidentified Flying Objects, December 2, 1952, DOC 0005515935.

[87] National Security Council Directive (Draft) "Unidentified Flying Objects," DOC 0005515935.

indicate an intent to continue to move along the path outlined in this draft NSC directive.

These memos were part of a flurry of activity in the first half of December 1952. CIA personnel were meeting with outside scientists, reviewing reports from other countries about UFO sightings, and raising the issue at interagency meetings. On December 4, 1952, the Intelligence Advisory Committee[88] met and discussed coordination of intelligence efforts for the UFO question. As a result, the Director of Central Intelligence will "(e)nlist the services of selected scientists to review and apprise the available evidence in the light of pertinent scientific theories."[89]

This decision to set up a scientific panel appears to conflict with the stated intent to have a quick review of a narrow question. As will be shown in succeeding chapters, the formation of a scientific panel did not conflict with the goal of a rapid assessment. After the scope of the study was determined in December 1952, CIA OSI quickly formed what came to be known as the Robertson Panel.

---

[88] The Intelligence Advisory Committee met regularly and was Chaired by the CIA Director. Membership includes high ranking intelligence officers from the State Department, each military branch, Atomic Energy Commission, CIA, and the FBI. The December 4, 1952, was chaired by Robert Armory, Acting Deputy Director (Intelligence) CIA.

[89] Intelligence Advisory Committee Meeting Minutes, December 4, 1952, 82-00400R000100050004-7.

CHAPTER SEVEN

"A DISTINGUISHED PANEL OF NON-MILITARY SCIENTISTS"[90]

On December 4, 1952, the Intelligence Advisory Committee recommended that the Director of Central Intelligence "(e)nlist the services of selected scientists to review and apprise the available evidence in the light of pertinent scientific theories."[91] This process, after delays during the fall of 1952, moved quickly with a panel of scientists chosen in December and early January 1953. The CIA's official history of the flying saucer era claims the scientific panel was made up of "non-military scientists."[92] However, the five scientists each worked on military weapons projects both before and after their service on the Robertson Panel. The majority moved back and forth from highly classified projects to academia during their careers. Atomic weapon development, radar applications, intelligence assessments, and other highly classified programs requiring scientific expertise were part of their assignments.

The work of the Robertson Panel, while circulated throughout the executive branch, was a classified secret. It did not become public knowledge until former Project Blue Book member, Captain

---

[90] Haines, Gerald K., "A Die-Hard Issue: CIA's Role in the Study of UFOs, 1947–90." https://www.cia.gov/resources/csi/studies-in-intelligence/studies-in-intelligence-1997/cias-role-in-the-study-of-ufos-1947-1990/.

[91] Intelligence Advisory Committee Meeting Minutes, December 4, 1952, 82-00400R000100050004-7.

[92] Haines, Gerald K., "A Die-Hard Issue: CIA's Role in the Study of UFOs, 1947–90."

Edward Ruppelt, disclosed that the Panel was formed but provided little details in his 1956 book.[93] The "non-military scientists" held security clearances and kept their secrets, including their paid relationships with the CIA. They were not disinterested scientists and their work on the Panel was hardly an academic role. Two of the panelists were part of a WWII effort to understand foo fighters, the forerunners to UFOs. As will be seen, the Panel took no independent investigatory steps. They only reviewed what the Air Force and the CIA wanted them to see. A pattern that continues to this day with the Office of the Director of National Intelligence, *Preliminary Assessment: Unidentified Aerial Phenomena* and the 2022 and 2023 ARRO annual reports.

Once the direction was established, DCI Walter Bedell Smith was to brief President Truman on the formation of the CIA scientific consultant group. On December 12, 1952, a CIA Deputy Directors meeting that included DCI Smith set the date of a meeting with President Truman for his briefing on flying saucers.[94]

On Friday, December 19, 1952, President Truman was briefed at 10:45 A.M. for a scheduled 15 minutes by DCI Smith. The President's military advisor, Admiral Sydney Souers, and James Lay, Jr., Executive Secretary of the National Security Council, were also present. Because of the delays, the scientific panel was not scheduled until the last week of the Truman Administration. This meant its report would go to the next administration.

With the December 19th approval, the Panel began to take shape. It consisted of five primary members. Three of the Panel members already had current consulting arrangements with the military and/or intelligence community. Two who did not have

---

[93] Ruppelt, E., *The Report on Unidentified Flying Objects*, readaclassic.com (2010), reprint of 1956 original version, pp. 190, 211–215.

[94] CIA Deputies Meeting Minutes, December 10, 1952, Document Release Date: January 23, 2020, Case Number: F-2018-01132.

current agreements were Dr. Luis Alvarez and Dr. Thornton Page. They were not on the list of approved CIA consultants. The panelists and consultants were paid at a rate of $50.00 per day. The requisition request was made on January 9, 1953, less than a week before the Panel was to start work. A CIA declassified document lists the panelists and other participants as follows:

SCIENTIFIC ADVISORY PANEL ON UNIDENTIFIED FLYING OBJECTS 14–17 JANUARY 1953

MEMBERS	ORGANIZATION	FIELD
Dr. H. P. Robertson (Chair)	California Institute of Tech	Physics, weapons systems
Dr. Luis W. Alvarez	University of California	Physics, radar
Lloyd V. Berkner	Associated Universities Inc.	Geophysics
Dr. Samuel Goudsmit	Brookhaven National Labs	Atomic structure, statistics
Dr. Thornton Page	Office of Research Operations, Johns Hopkins University	Astronomy, Astrophysics
ASSOCIATE MEMBERS		
Dr. J. Allen Hynek	Ohio State University	Astronomy
Mr. Frederick C. Durant	Arthur D. Little, Inc.	Rockets, guided missiles
INTERVIEWEES		
Brig. Gen. William M. Garland	Commanding General, ATIC	Scientific and technical intelligence
Dr. H. Marshall Chadwell	Assistant Director, O/SI, CIA	Scientific and technical intelligence
Mr. Ralph L. Clark	Deputy Assistant Director, O/SI, CIA	Scientific and technical intelligence

Others attended the meetings but are not listed. Lloyd Berkner presents some mysteries about the Panel's workings. He was listed as a member in most declassified documents. However, some declassified documents still have his name redacted. Other declassified documents fail to list him as a participant at all. Those documents elevate Air Force Consultant Dr. J. Allen Hynek from associate member to a full panelist in his place. Declassified documents indicate that Berkner did not attend most of the sessions but, along with CIA staff, wrote the report, which was submitted to the Panel for final editing. In response to follow-up correspondence, panelist Dr. Samuel Goudsmit did not even recall that Berkner participated. It is quite curious that the initial author of the report did not participate in most of the Panel's deliberations. Yet, he wrote the report behind the scenes with CIA staff while the Panel was in session.

Dr. Harold Percy Robertson

Dr. H.P. "Bob" Robertson (1903–1961) was chosen as chair of the Panel. With his scientific, military, and intelligence connections, he was perfectly suited to carry out the mission of the Panel. For most of his career, he shuffled between academia, military, and intelligence matters. He was at the center of many significant military-scientific issues from World War II forward.

Dr. Robertson was a physicist with an undergraduate degree in mathematics (1922) and a master's degree in mathematics and physics (1923) from the University of Washington. He received his doctorate from California Institute of Technology (Cal Tech) (1925) in mathematics and physics. Robertson taught at Cal Tech from 1927 to 1929. From 1929 to 1947, he was a professor at Princeton University. He returned to Cal Tech as a professor in mathematical physics from 1947 until his untimely death (auto accident) in 1961.

His main academic interests were in differential geometry and group theory. He applied his mathematics expertise to problems in atomic physics, cosmology, quantum physics, and general relativity. He associated with some of the best minds in science, such as Albert Einstein, John Von Newmann, Leopold Infeld, and Vannevar Bush. In 1939, he began work on defense issues that would continue for the rest of his life.

During World War II, Robertson served in a variety of capacities. He worked out of the London office of the Office of Scientific Research and Development on a variety of projects, including serving as liaison to several clandestine efforts to gather information on German weapons development. One of his assignments was the study of foo fighters. Foo fighters were forerunners to flying saucers. They followed airplanes in both the Pacific and European theaters during World War II. Each side thought they were secret weapons from the other side.[95] "Bob" Robertson was also Chief of the Scientific Advisory Section at Supreme Headquarters of the Allied Expeditionary Force. For his service, he was awarded the Order of Merit (1946).

After the war, he continued to work on defense and intelligence-related scientific problems for the United States government. He was a CIA employee/consultant during the initial post-war period prior to being appointed to chair the Panel. From 1950 to 1952, Dr. Robertson was director of the Secretary of Defense's Weapon Systems Evaluation Group.

After his short service on the CIA scientific panel, Robertson continued his work with the military. He was the first Chairman of the Defense Science Board (1956–1961). This board was formed to give the Secretary of Defense advice and counsel about scientific, technical, manufacturing, and related issues. Prior to his

---

[95] https://timesmachine.nytimes.com/timesmachine/1945/01/02/issue.html

appointment as the initial Chair of the Defense Science Board, he was the science advisor to the NATO Supreme Allied Commander Europe in 1954 and 1955. Coincidentally, this was a time of high UFO activity over Europe. In 1954, it was estimated that 58.4% of all reported UFO sightings in the world occurred in Europe. In October 1954 alone, there were 961 (83.6%) reported European sightings out of 1,150 worldwide. It was quite likely that Dr. Robertson used his foo fighter and Robertson Panel background in Europe as the science advisor to the Supreme Commander of NATO when it had a huge influx of reported sightings.

Dr. Luis W. Alvarez

Dr. Alvarez (1911–1988) was chosen Vice Chairman of the Panel. He received his undergraduate degree (1932), master's degree (1934), and doctorate (1936) at the University of Chicago, all in physics. Alvarez joined the University of California (Berkeley) faculty, first as a research associate and later as a professor, in 1936. Among his many early accomplishments, he co-discovered the radioactivity of tritium, a source of thermonuclear energy.

During World War II, he worked at MIT on radar systems for the military. He contributed to advancements in the microwave early warning system, the Eagle high-altitude bombing system and the ground-control landing approach system. From 1944 to 45, Alvarez worked at the Los Alamos Laboratory, where he developed the detonators for setting off the first two atomic bombs (Alamogordo, July 16, 1945, and Hiroshima, August 6, 1945). Alvarez was one of the scientists that investigated foo fighters on behalf of the Army Air Corps, though little is known about these efforts. After the war, he returned to Cal Berkeley.

After his service on the CIA Robertson Panel, Professor Alvarez continued to work on scientific breakthroughs. In 1968, he won the Nobel Prize in Physics. The Nobel Committee stated his recognition was: "for his decisive contributions to elementary particle physics, in particular the discovery of a large number of resonance states, made possible through his development of the technique of using hydrogen bubble chamber and data analysis."[96]

Perhaps his most famous discovery was made with the help of his son, Walter Alvarez, a geologist. Walter discussed a problem in his research with his father related to a boundary in rock formations formed about 65 million years ago. Professor Luis Alvarez found the grey rock layer contained iridium, a common element in meteorites. This layer was formed at the same time around the world. The Alvarez duo theorized that this record demonstrated that the mass extinction of the dinosaurs was caused by a massive meteorite hitting the Earth. Their theory was hotly contested, but two years after Dr. Luis Alvarez's death in 1988, the massive crater off the Yucatan Peninsula was discovered and dated to match their theory.[97]

Lloyd Viel Berkner

Mr. Berkner (1905–1967) was a physicist who shuffled between government and academia his entire adult life. He was born in Milwaukee, Wisconsin and graduated from the University of Minnesota in 1927. From his graduation, he immediately embarked on a scientific career that took him, literally, to the ends of the earth. Berkner never had time to do post-graduate work in geophysics. However, he was on the leading edge of research while in school and thereafter.

Mr. Berkner was interested in radios, and, in addition to his electrical engineering studies, he combined his passion for radios with his passion for flying. As a member of the Naval Reserve, he developed and tested a VHF radio for naval aircraft while still in school. After graduation, Berkner went to work for the U.S. Bureau of Lighthouses, working on radio beacons for the Airways Division.

---

[96] https://www.nobelprize.org/nobel_prizes/physics/laureates/1968/.

[97] https://www.famousscientists.org/luis-alvarez/.

He also worked with Admiral Byrd in the Antarctic to set up radio communication equipment needed for Byrd's expedition.[98]

In 1930, after his work with Byrd, he returned to the Bureau of Lighthouses and was able to gain a half-million dollars in funding for studies of the ionosphere, using the recently developed radio-pulse technology. In 1933, Berkner joined the Department of Terrestrial Magnetism (DTM) at Carnegie Institution of Washington (CIW), which had developed radio-pulse technology. While at DTM, Berkner traveled the world to work on projects with some of the finest scientific minds of the time as well as meeting CIW's President Dr. Vannevar Bush. Dr. Bush, with war on the horizon, convinced the Roosevelt Administration to form the National Defense Research Committee (NDRC), later renamed the Office of Scientific Research and Development (OSRD). Berkner was appointed as Bush's assistant. However, in September 1941, Berkner was recalled to active naval duty. In the Navy, he worked on radar development and received several honors for his wartime work.

After the war, he returned to DTM. His return was to be short-lived as Dr. Vannevar Bush appointed him to be the Secretary of the Research and Development Board that had been formed by the War Department and the Navy. It's Chairman, Vannevar Bush, once again turned to Berkner for an important defense research position. Dr. Bush once spoke about Berkner:

> "Lloyd V. Berkner was undoubtedly one of the best-liked men in the whole field of science and engineering. He played a significant role in the scientific effort of World War II and, after it, in the explosive development of public funding for science and technology. At the same time, he made major

---

[98] https://www.nap.edu/read/2037/chapter/3#4.

contributions to geophysics and to the development of international cooperation in science."[99]

The cooperation between these men would continue on defense issues. His appointment to the Robertson Panel was likely, due in part, to the support of Bush.

Many believe that the two shared more than a public collaboration. In 1984, Jamie Shandera, a television producer, received undeveloped film that contained pictures showing alleged classified documents of a secret committee formed by President Truman to deal with the issues associated with a flying saucer crash in the New Mexico desert near Roswell Army Air Force Base in 1947. The documents were claimed to be a manual for an alleged secret committee, Majestic 12 (MJ-12). Those who have researched these document copies believe them to be real and point to a corroborating letter found in government archives.[100] The current Air Force website claims MJ-12 did not exist.[101] The contested documents show that Dr. Vannevar Bush and Lloyd Berkner were members of MJ-12.

Whether or not such a committee existed, it is likely that Dr. Bush and Lloyd Berkner would have been involved in any top-secret study of the flying saucer problem. Bush was the most influential scientist on defense issues under the Roosevelt and Truman Administrations, before and after World War II. Berkner was chosen by Bush to be his administrative/scientific support on defense-related issues before World War II and after. It is not surprising, with his background, that Lloyd Berkner would be at the center of flying saucer research. His knowledge of radar and the

---

[99] Lloyd Viel Berkner—A Commentary, *IEEE Spectrum,* 1967 https://www.nap.edu/read/2037/chapter/3.

[100] Friedman, Stanton, *TOP SECRET/MAJIC*, 1997, Marlowe & Co.

[101] https://www.archives.gov/research/military/air-force/ufos.

ionosphere would be valuable to any study of unknown aerial phenomenon.

In 1951, after several government scientific assignments, including a stint as the science advisor to the U.S. Secretary of State and preliminary work on NATO, Berkner became President of Associated Universities Incorporated (AUI). AUI was formed by nine northeastern colleges to establish and operate a nuclear research center. He served as president until 1960.

He was also instrumental in establishing global cooperation among scientists. Berkner was the prime mover behind the International Geophysical Year in 1957-58. Later, he went on to work in the southwest to establish a graduate research center in Texas. His work was never completed as heart problems resulted in a premature passing in 1967.

Dr. Samuel Goudsmit

Dr. Goudsmit (1902–1978) was born in The Hague, Netherlands. He studied physics and gained a PhD in 1927 at the University of Leiden. He emigrated to the United States and was a professor at the University of Michigan from 1927 to 1946. Goudsmit had breaks in service to work at MIT on nuclear research for the World War II war effort. He was appointed the chief scientific member of the Alsos Mission that went into Nazi-occupied territory to contact German nuclear physicists and learn about Nazi progress towards building a nuclear weapon. He was not part of the Manhattan Project to keep him from gaining special knowledge in case of capture. Sadly, while he was performing his wartime duties, his parents were killed in a Nazi concentration camp.

After the war, he spent one year teaching at Northwestern University before joining the Brookhaven National Laboratory. From 1952 to 1960, Dr. Goudsmit chaired the physics department at Brookhaven. This was a key position in government. Atomic energy and weapon development were of the highest priority at the time. The work was highly classified and had many military applications.

For the last four years of his life, he was on the faculty of the University of Nevada (Reno). One interesting aspect of his life was that he was an Egyptologist. Although it was merely his passion, Dr. Goudsmit devoted much of his time studying and writing scholarly articles on the subject. The Samuel A. Goudsmit Collection of Egyptian Antiquities is still at the Kelsey Museum of Archeology at the University of Michigan, where he was on the physics faculty for almost 20 years.

Dr. Thornton Page

Dr. Thornton L. Page (1913–1996) was added to the Robertson Panel on January 9th, less than a week before it began meeting. While he was not a consultant having a preexisting contract with the CIA, he was a professor of astronomy at Johns Hopkins University in nearby Maryland.

Page received his undergraduate degree in physics at Yale University in 1934. He received his doctorate at Oxford University (1938) in astrophysics. Soon thereafter, he served in the Pacific Theater during World War II. After the war, he became an astrophysics professor (1946–1950) at the University of Chicago. Next, he joined Johns Hopkins University (1950–1958) to work on its contract with the U.S. Army at the Operations Research Office.

In 1958, Dr. Page returned to teaching as the head of the astronomy department at Wesleyan University. He remained there until 1971. During his tenure, he took leave to teach at UCLA (1964), Yale (1966), Harvard-Smithsonian Observatory (1965–67) (space tracking program), and to NASA (1968), lecturing astronauts on astronomy.

In 1971, Dr. Page returned to the Navy as a member of the Naval Research Laboratory until retirement in 1976. As with other members of the Robertson Panel, he moved back and forth between academia and military research.

Frederick C. Durant, III

Frederick Durant (1916–2015) was a consultant to the CIA on missile issues. Along with Lloyd Berkner, he participated in writing the draft report that was presented to the Panel on the third of four days of Panel meetings. Many declassified documents refer to the Robertson Panel Report as the Durant Report, which emphasizes his contribution as panel secretary and associate member.

Durant graduated from Lehigh University in engineering in 1939. After a brief stint at E.I. du Pont de Nemours & Co., he enlisted in the Navy and served as a pilot. After the war, he went to work for Bell Aircraft Corporation (1946–1947). From 1948 to 1951, he was director of engineering for the Naval Air Rocket Test Station. During the Korean War, he returned to the military as a test pilot.

While working with the CIA as a consultant in 1953, he was elected president of the American Rocket Society. He worked on various space programs during the 1950s, including work that led to the United States' first successful satellite launch (Explorer I, 1958). In 1964, the Smithsonian hired him as assistant director and head of the newly formed Astronautics Department to organize the National Air and Space Museum. He retired in 1980.

Dr. Josef Allen Hynek

Dr. J. Allen Hynek (1910–1986) was an astronomer who was under contract with the Air Force to assist in the investigation of flying saucers, primarily under the aegis of Project Blue Book (1952–1969). He received his undergraduate degree (1935) and doctorate from the University of Chicago. He started teaching at Ohio State University (1936) in the Physics and Astronomy Department.

During World War II, he worked at Johns Hopkins in the Applied Physics Laboratory. Hynek contributed to the development of the radio proximity fuse. After the war, he returned to Ohio State University, becoming a full professor in 1950. Down the road from Ohio State was Wright-Patterson Air Force Base, where the ATIC was located. Prior to Project Blue Book, the Air Force had two programs: Project Sign (1947–1949) and Project Grudge (1949–1952) that investigated public flying saucer reports.

In 1948, the Air Force retained J. Allen Hynek as a scientific consultant. He stayed with the various public programs until Project Blue Book ended in 1969. Over time, he gradually became more accepting of the reality of UFOs. However, at the time of the Robertson Panel, he was an interested skeptic. As an associate member of the Panel, he mostly served in a staff role, participating in various briefings and presentations. Even though some documents listed him as a full member and omitted the role of Lloyd Berkner, he was not allowed to make a significant contribution to the proceedings.

In the same year as the Robertson Panel, he prepared a report on brightness fluctuations of stars. This report was a forerunner to the work that predicts the location of planets in other star systems based on the changes in brightness when a planet transits the star. After the Robertson Panel, he continued his dual role as a professor of astronomy and Air Force consultant. In 1960, he joined the Northwestern University faculty as Astronomy Department Chair. In 1973, having come full circle about the reality of UFOs, he founded the Center for UFO Studies (CUFOS). Hynek died in 1986.

All the chosen panelists, full and associate, had worked on classified military programs prior to their service on the Panel. Each knew the concern over the growth in the Soviet threat and was accustomed to keeping military secrets. All contributed to science and were well respected members of the scientific community. As with much of the CIA's public information about its involvement in the UFO "problem," calling these men "civilian scientists" was consistent with the Agency's efforts to downplay its long-term involvement.

CHAPTER EIGHT

ROBERTSON PANEL DELIBERATIONS

The CIA Robertson Panel met at a crucial juncture in history when a leadership change altered the way the CIA operated during the Truman/Eisenhower transition. The first session was held on Wednesday morning, January 14th, and the last on Saturday afternoon, the 17th. Some official documents incorrectly list meetings through the 18th. By Tuesday of the next week, Dwight David Eisenhower was sworn in as the 34th President of the United States.

The Eisenhower Administration's new director of the CIA (DCI) was Allen Dulles. Dulles was not trusted by Truman and had been passed over for the CIA's top job. Rather than going through DCI Walter Bedell Smith, the Robertson Panel Report would go through Dulles. The change in administration brought a change of direction for the intelligence community. Dulles's experience during World War II in clandestine activities foreshadowed the new CIA emphasis on clandestine action rather than emphasizing passive intelligence gathering. Aggressive measures used during wartime became the norm during the Cold War. While there were exceptions, the Truman Administration's CIA had emphasized intelligence gathering.

Allen Dulles's brother, John Foster Dulles, was confirmed as Eisenhower's new Secretary of State. John Foster brought a vision that saw the world only through the lens of the struggle to defeat communism. Every region of the world was seen through this prism. Nuances based on a local country's unique situation were largely ignored. The Dulles brothers, as heads of the State Department and

CIA, could take a more aggressive approach in the developing Cold War. Each country had to pick a side. A country's adherence to democratic principles took a back seat to the war on communism.[102]

This change in emphasis would play a role in how the CIA approached domestic issues. Many of the excesses of the CIA began with this new approach to real and perceived threats. The formation of the Robertson Panel was the result of a White House referral over domestic concerns about the 1952 flying saucer wave, which included buzzing the White House. While originally the idea was for a scientific review of the phenomenon, the change in mission affected the charge to the Robertson Panel. First, its formation was delayed until mid-December 1952. After a White House meeting between President Truman and CIA Director Walter Bedell Smith on December 19th, the referral took on added urgency. However, the focus changed from an actual objective scientific analysis into a Cold War threat assessment. It was no longer a study about the source of the phenomenon.

Opening Day: Wednesday, January 14, 1953 (Morning Session)

Four of five panelists were present for the opening session.[103] Mr. Lloyd Berkner was not present until part way through the sixth

---

[102] Kinzer, Stephen, *The Two Brothers: John Foster Dulles, Allen Dulles and Their Secret World War*, Henry Holt and Company (2013); Talbot, David, *The Devil's Chessboard*: Dulles, Allen, *the CIA, and the Rise of America's Secret Government*, Harper Perennial (2015).

[103] The Wednesday morning attendees were Chair Dr. Harold Percy Robertson, member Dr. Luis Alvarez, member Dr. Thornton Page, member Dr. Samuel Goudsmit, CIA official Philip G. Strong, Lt. Col. Frederick C.E. Oder (CIA Physics & Engineering Division), David B. Stevenson (W & E Division), Frederick Durant (CIA consultant and panel secretary) and Marshall Chadwell (CIA Assistant Director Office of Scientific Intelligence). Philip G. Strong is listed in the Panel Report as "Mr." However, Strong was a Marine Corps officer who served in various intelligence functions until his retirement in 1964 at the rank of Brigadier General. The 1947 National Security Act, forming the CIA,

of eight sessions (Friday afternoon). Instead of attending the proceedings, Mr. Berkner helped write the draft report. The draft report was based on the recommendations that the Air Force and CIA had agreed to months earlier.

The meeting was opened by CIA Assistant Director for Scientific Intelligence (AD/SI) Marshall Chadwell. He reviewed the Agency's actions taken to establish the Panel. He then discussed the "potential dangers to national security related to these sightings."[104] CIA's Philip Strong then elaborated on the "indirect" potential dangers of the sightings by American citizens. By "indirect," CIA staff focused their presentation on the dangers posed by persons who report UFOs. After the initial staff presentation, AD/SI Dr. Chadwell turned the proceedings over to Chair Robertson.

Chair Dr. Harold P. Robertson (Cal Tech) discussed the evidence selected to be shared with the Panel by the CIA and Air Force. Certain panelists received evidence individually, with radar case histories routed to physicist Dr. Alvarez, who had helped develop military radar during World War II. Astronomer Dr. Thornton Page was tasked with visual sighting cases such as the green fireballs, only seen over New Mexico defense installations for a short time (1948). The declassified version of the Robertson Panel Report does not go into detail about the specifics of the materials supplied to the panelists before this first session.

The record does show that no eyewitnesses were ever brought in front of the Panel, despite numerous reports by military personnel and other trained observers. The morning session concluded by showing two movies. One taken by a naval

---

specifically allowed active duty military personnel to keep their military rank while working for the CIA.

[104] *Report of Scientific Advisory Panel on Unidentified Flying Objects, Convened by Office of Scientific Intelligence CIA,* January 14–18 (sic), 1953 p. 2, www.nicap.org/reports/1953_robertson_panel.htm. Copies in the CIA Archive are mostly illegible.

photographic specialist with his personal 16 mm movie camera (Tremonton, Utah: July 2, 1952). The other was taken by a minor league baseball executive who filmed UFOs and a military jet travelling near the local ballpark (Great Falls, Montana: August 15, 1950).

Nick Mariana, the general manager of the Great Falls Electrics minor league baseball team, filmed his sighting with a 16 mm camera. At the request of Air Force representatives, he turned over his original film for analysis. When he got his film back, he noticed that significant portions of the film had been removed. The parts removed showed the UFO at close range. All he got back from the Air Force was footage of the objects at a distance. It is not known whether the unedited footage was shown to the Robertson Panel.

The Tremonton, Utah film was taken by a naval photographer, Warrant Officer D.C. Newhouse.[105] He had been transferred and was driving his family to his new assignment in Oregon when he took the movies. The current public version shows multiple glowing objects at a distance. According to Delbert Newhouse, the "frames of the movie showing a single UFO moving away over the horizon were missing when the film was returned."[106] The missing footage would have helped establish the distance of the object from the camera that would aid its analysis. We do not know which version was seen by the Panel.

The morning session lasted two and one-half hours. The Panel Report does not discuss what "potential dangers to national security related to these sightings," were discussed. However, the report indicates that the security concerns related to "indirect" effects of the sightings, not from UFOs. The initial session adjourned at noon.

---

[105] https://www.ufocasebook.com/tremontonutah.html.

[106] Ibid.

Opening Day: Wednesday, January 14, 1953 (Afternoon Session)

The afternoon session began at 2:00 P.M. Two members of the Naval Photo Interpretation Laboratory, Washington, D.C., joined the Panel and gave the naval lab's analysis of the Tremonton and Great Falls films. The naval personnel reported that the objects in the Tremonton film were self-luminous and could not be birds. The movement exhibited in the films did not change the degree of luminosity that a flight of birds would exhibit. As birds fly, their movements change the angle of view from the perspective of the witness, causing the luminosity to vary. The objects filmed show consistent brightness throughout their flight.[107]

Despite the professional opinion of the Naval Photo Interpretation Laboratory, the panelists found that the films showed mundane objects. The record indicates that much debate took place over the Navy's findings. The Navy's presentation and subsequent discussion lasted approximately 2 ½ hours. Neither of the movies' photographers were present. Ultimately, the Robertson Panel disregarded the Navy's findings and determined that the objects were birds (Tremonton) and aircraft (Great Falls).[108]As discussed earlier, both photographers stated that their films were returned with critical portions removed. The question is whether the Panel saw the unredacted versions of the two films? If redactions were made, were they made before or after they were analyzed by the Navy photo lab? The redactions made to the Tremonton film would not have affected the luminosity of the objects flying away from the camera even if other critical information was removed.

---

[107] https://www.youtube.com/watch?v=qKlszbnZx3o (Tremonton, Utah and the Great Falls, Montana Films, edited versions).

[108] Ruppelt, Edward J., *The Report on Unidentified Flying Objects*, (Original 1956 Edition) Doubleday & Company (1956), reissued Cosimo Classics (2011), reprint of 1956 original version, pp. 211–215.

For the last portion of the Wednesday deliberations, the Panel heard from Air Force Captain Edward J. Ruppelt about the procedures for handling and evaluating sightings. Captain Ruppelt, head of the newly formed Project Blue Book, was stationed at Wright-Patterson Air Force Base, Ohio. Blue Book was a small branch of the Advanced Technical Intelligence Center (ATIC), which also evaluated terrestrial foreign military technology. Captain Ruppelt then discussed efforts to improve the quality of reports. The Panel adjourned at 5:15 P.M.

Day Two: Thursday, January 15, 1953 (Morning Session)

Day two started with Captain Ruppelt still reviewing the investigatory methods employed by Project Blue Book. He was followed by ATIC (Blue Book) consultant Dr. J. Allen Hynek. He described Project Stork to the Panel. Project Stork was an analysis ordered by Ruppelt in 1952 to review and categorize UFO sightings from 1947 through 1952 in order to make sense of numerous sighting reports.[109] It was contracted out to the Battelle Memorial Institute who used early computers to categorize reports. Later, Battelle's Report was issued by the Air Force as Special Report Number 14.[110]

According to the declassified records, the Panel never went into serious detail about the findings of Project Stork. In its later form as Special Report Number 14, the percentage of sightings classified as "unknown" was 25%, an alarming number to dismiss without further explanation. A separate category contained over 30% of sightings where insufficient data made clear that the "unknown" category contained reports with sufficient data for analysis. These numbers were unknown to the public for decades. During the 1950s, the Secretary of the Air Force characterized Special Report Number 14's data as only having 3% unknown.

---

[109] www.cufon.org/cufon/stork1-7.htm.

[110] https://www.ufocasebook.com/pdf/specialreport14.pdf.

While this claim helped calm the public, it misrepresented the results of the report.

The record of the Panel's proceedings appears to show that the focus was on the process for collecting reports or what threats arose because people reported flying saucers. The record of the proceedings does indicate that some case histories were discussed in detail, but no information was provided as to the quality or type of sightings reviewed. Except for the two films, few of the actual cases reviewed were mentioned in the Panel Report. No eyewitnesses were called before the Panel. Finally, the Thursday morning session ended with a film of seagulls in flight.

Day Two: Thursday, January 15, 1953 (Afternoon Session)

The afternoon began with Air Force Lt. Col. Oder giving a briefing on Project Twinkle (Air Force Meteorological Research Center, Cambridge, Massachusetts). Twinkle was an attempt to have 24-hour-a-day photographic monitoring to take UFO pictures. Oder discussed the problems with the program which used fixed cameras. It required the cooperation of the UFOs, who had to fly in front of the cameras. The program was a failure.

At 4:15 P.M., Brig. Gen. William M. Garland joined the Panel with Assistant Director for Scientific Intelligence Marshall Chadwell. Garland had recently been appointed the commanding officer at the Advanced Technical Intelligence Center, which housed Project Blue Book. General Garland offered personal opinions as follows:

> "a. That greater use of Air Force intelligence officers in the field (for follow-up investigation) appeared desirable, but that they required thorough briefing.
>
> b. That vigorous effort should be made to declassify as many of the reports as possible.

c. That some increase in the ATIC section devoted to U.F.O. analysis was indicated."[111]

General Garland advocated devoting more resources to the UFO problem. He also wanted the public to have better access to the data. After his presentation, the Panel adjourned at 5:00 P.M. The Panel Report did not address any of his recommendations.

Day Three: Friday, January 16, 1953 (Morning Session)

As the Panel opened its Friday morning session, they spent an hour generally discussing the issues and reference materials. One paper, prepared by Dr. J. Allen Hynek, was read to the Panel with Hynek's observations and conclusions. At the time, early in his involvement with the phenomenon, Dr. Hynek was a skeptic who tried to keep an open mind about the subject. After he finished, the Panel heard from Major Dewey Fournet about case histories and his personal conclusions. Specifics about these presentations are not available in a declassified form. Finally, Fournet, Hynek, and Ruppelt went over additional case histories before the adjournment for lunch.

Day Three: Friday, January 16, 1953 (Afternoon Session)

At 2:00 P.M., the Panel reconvened with CIA personnel and Dr. Hynek present. Panel member Mr. Lloyd Berkner joined the group for the first time. Rather than listening to the evidence, he had been working with CIA staff to draft the Panel's report.

The Panel discussed the various presentations and came to general conclusions. The Panel recommended that the Chair draft a report to the Panel for presentation the next morning. Once completed, the report would be forwarded to the CIA's Assistant

---

[111] *Report of Scientific Advisory Panel on Unidentified Flying Objects Convened by Office of Scientific Intelligence CIA*, January 14–18, 1953, p. 4–5, www.nicap.org/reports/1953_robertson_panel.htm.

Director of Scientific Intelligence Marshall Chadwell. The declassified record of the proceedings does not mention any of the conclusions reached on Friday.

Day Four: Saturday, January 17, 1953 (Morning Session)

At 9:45 A.M., the Panel's final day began. The Chairman submitted a draft report to the group. The declassified version of the report notes that, while the chair was tasked with writing the draft report Friday afternoon, the draft "had been reviewed and approved earlier by Dr. Berkner."[112] In other words, even though the Panel tasked the Chair to write the draft Panel Report, it had already been drafted by CIA staff and Mr. Berkner. Director of Intelligence Marshall Chadwell and the Air Force had stated their approval of the draft report.

Day Four: Saturday, January 17, 1953 (Afternoon Session)

The final session was held on Saturday afternoon and dealt with minor rewording of the draft report. Since individual recommendations of Panel members were not included in the Panel Report, a separate internal report was sent to the assistant director of scientific intelligence that contained Panel member comments. The declassified version of the Panel Report has their comments and suggestions in part II. The tab that contains the actual report is short and merely summarizes the overall conclusions. In a nutshell, the Panel Report recommends the same conclusions that the CIA and Air Force came up with months before the Panel was convened. The only independent conclusion of the Panel was a public education component of the Panel's "debunking" policy recommendation.

---

[112] Ibid @ p. 6.

CHAPTER NINE

ROBERTSON PANEL FINDINGS

The Panel's report was circulated to interested agencies of the Eisenhower Administration. Versions of the findings are now part of the declassified record, but we still do not know whether it was ever formally made a classified regulatory policy.[113] Various versions have different language, but none have the full report available. As will be shown, later declassified documents and public actions of the government show that the recommendations have been followed until recently.

The actual Robertson Panel Report, also referred to as the Durant Report, was only three pages long and contains cryptic, generalized findings. The Panel Report's only finding on the UFO phenomenon itself was as follows:

> "That the evidence presented on Unidentified Flying Objects shows no indication that these phenomenon constitute a direct physical threat to national security."[114]

While the Panel never attempted to identify the phenomenon, it found that it wasn't a "direct" threat. This finding about the

---

[113] In October 1952, the Air Force and CIA staffs agreed that their goal would be to minimize the amount of paperwork in this endeavor. The lack of paperwork reduced the ability to later scrutinize the Panel's conclusions. "Flying Saucers Problem," October 14, 1952, CIA-RDP81R00560R000100020010-9.pdf.

[114] "Report of Scientific Advisory Panel on Unidentified Flying Objects Convened by Office of Scientific Intelligence CIA," January 14–18 (sic) 1953, Tab "A" NICAP Declassified Version: www.nicap.org/reports/1953_robertson_panel.htm.

capabilities and intent of UFOs did not deviate from then-existing Air Force policy. While there were "unknown" cases, the Panel found that, given enough information, all sightings could be explained by 1953-era science.

In coming to this conclusion, the Panel never interviewed a single eyewitness. It never sought additional information about cases specified as "unknown" after Air Force investigation. As discussed earlier, the "unknown" category in the Air Force Special Report Number 14 only contained reports that had enough information needed to draw a conclusion. Reports that lacked necessary information were listed in the "insufficient data" category. The Robertson Panel never talked to trained observers, such as commercial airline or military pilots, who actually witnessed the phenomenon firsthand. There were highly credible reports from airline pilots that, if the Panel wanted to understand the phenomenon, could have been called before the Panel. The Robertson Panel concentrated on 15 cases, only eight of which are specifically referred to in declassified versions of the Panel Report.

With regard to the Naval analysis of the Tremonton and Great Falls sightings films, the Panel disputed the opinions of the photographic experts. One must wonder how the Naval Photo Interpretation Laboratory failed to recognize "birds" or "planes" in films shot by a professional military photographer and an experienced amateur photographer. The findings were a poor reflection on the expertise of the professionals in the military laboratory charged with detecting threats and keeping the country safe.

Nine years later, the country almost went to war over photographic evidence analyzed by one who reviewed the two films. During the 1962 Cuban Missile Crisis, Arthur Lundahl, a former naval intelligence photo interpretive expert, gave critical advice to President Kennedy. However, according to the Robertson Panel, President Kennedy relied upon an expert who could not tell a bird from a self-luminous object. The Panel's report merely concludes naval experts were wrong without giving any serious explanation of the rejection of the Navy's expert opinion. Assuming that both photographers' claims of missing footage are true, we don't even know whether the Panel saw unredacted versions of the films.

Despite the cavalier way the Panel treated the evidence, the more disturbing part of the recommendations related to the Panel's determination of the "real" threats. The threat did not come from UFOs themselves; it came from American citizens who have either seen or study flying saucers. They constitute "a threat to the orderly functioning of the protective organs of the body politic." The government itself was threatened by these beliefs. This threat was based on the premise that citizens would see fake UFOs, call the Air Force public phone lines, and prevent warnings of an imminent attack from other civilians. The real "threat" came from citizens who studied UFOs, helping create a "morbid national psychology."

However, the Panel had no evidence of UFO sightings created havoc or disrupted military preparedness. There was no evidence that civilian UFO organizations had subversive motives. No evidence of any UFO organization having any connections with the Soviet Union. No evidence of any effort to mislead the government or sow discontent. The Panel specifically called out two UFO organizations as being suspicious. One organization mentioned, the Civilian Flying Saucer Investigators (Los Angeles) (CSI-LA), conducted volunteer investigations using scientists and engineers who were working on defense projects, many from North American Aviation. These volunteers held security clearances. They were hardly the type that one would think possess a "harmful distrust of duly constituted authority."

As to panic being used to mask a surprise attack, there was no evidence to justify the conclusion. Except for speculation by the panelists, fueled by Air Force and CIA staff, there was no evidence presented and no expertise on the Panel to justify making this recommendation. Except for the 65 case studies (only 15 were reviewed in detail), the Panel spent most of its time reviewing procedures of how the Air Force investigated sightings. Little attention was paid to the obvious flaws in the fake UFO invasion theory.

At the time, the Air Force relied upon the civilian Ground Observer Corp to report air incursions over the United States. It was originally formed during World War II but restarted in 1950 to help with the new Cold War threat. The Corp had 75,000 members nationwide who received training in aircraft identification. It was disbanded in 1958, no longer necessary for detecting potential threats.

The Soviets did not deploy intercontinental ballistic missiles (ICBM) until 1959. In early 1954, the United States and Canada started installing the Distant Early Warning Line (DEW) in Canada and Alaska. It was a picket line of radar installations that would warn of a Soviet air attack from land-based bombers. The DEW Line was fully operational by 1957.

Prior to full operation of the DEW Line, the threat was slow-moving propeller-driven Soviet bombers. Their flight path would be over Canada and/or Alaska. It would take hours for the bombers to reach mainland U.S. territory. Reliance on continental mainland U.S. civilian spotters would be too late. By the time the bombers reached the 48 states, they would have flown over locations having radar. The likelihood of phone lines jamming was remote at best. Even if true, the civilian observers would have had a dedicated telephone line or radio communications. Since the observers were already trained in aircraft identification, the civilian observers, as a group, should not be fooled by manmade flying saucers.

With a Panel made up of military scientists, they held positions that could have been cleared to be updated about the DEW Line and its completion date. However, the Panel's recommendations had no time limitations tied to completion of the early warning system. Considering these factors, there was no evidence for a citizen panic/false flag operation scenario.

The potential psychological warfare implications were made by a Panel that had no expertise in mass psychology. No presentations were ever made to the Panel by experts in mass public behavior. All the scientists were physical scientists who worked on classified defense programs. The social science aspects of a "morbid national psychology" that would result in "hysterical behavior" were made up out of whole cloth.

In the Panel's background findings, there was no indication of Soviet efforts for a UFO "false flag" operation. However, this lack of evidence was cited as being sinister and meant the Soviets must be cooking things up. The Report's recommendation to squelch discussion of the topic was based on an implausible scenario. It was a solution looking for a problem.

On the flip side of the coin, the CIA and Air Force desires to use UFOs as an offensive weapon suffered from similar hurdles. The Panel Report found that there was no Soviet UFO press coverage at the time. It would be hard to use UFOs to stir up panic when most of the Soviet public had never heard of them. The CIA also did not have any human assets in the U.S.S.R. to launch this type of operation. This idea lacked any practical chance of succeeding.

A simpler reading of Soviet intentions would be that the lack of coverage was intentional. Perhaps, the Soviets were as worried about lack of control over the phenomenon as was our government. Why publicize a phenomenon that you do not control? In fact, the classified records that became public after the fall of the Soviet Union show the same governmental concern about the phenomenon as found in the United States.

In addition to the short final conclusions, the Panel prepared a section on the "Comments and Suggestions of the Panel."[115] This part explained the findings. It reiterated that nothing about the phenomenon was beyond the reach of 1953 science. While some military experts were concerned about the UFO phenomenon, the Panel had no such concern. It is an interesting scientific conclusion. Today, AARO still has no idea who is the source behind these objects. Yet in 1953, five CIA-chosen scientists had it all figured out.

Under "Comments and Suggestions," they also dismissed two expert sources that had concerns about UFOs. While none of the Panel were photographic experts, the Panel swept aside the conclusions of the Naval Photo Interpretation Laboratory. The Panel also dismissed the testimony of Major Dewey Fournet, former head of the Air Force's UFO study group. They dismissed his conclusions as follows:

> "Mr. Fournet, in his presentation, showed how he had eliminated each of the known and probable causes of sightings, leaving him 'extra-terrestrial' as the only one remaining in many cases. Fournet's background as an aeronautical engineer and technical intelligence officer (Project Officer, BLUEBOOK for 15 months) could not be slighted. However, the Panel could not accept any of the cases cited by him because they were raw, unevaluated reports."

The dismissal of the investigations conducted by "an aeronautical engineer and technical intelligence officer" was done because they were "raw and unevaluated." Yet, Fournet reached his conclusions after eliminating other causes. He did an evaluation of

---

[115] Comments and Suggestions, CIA DOC 0000015458. Even though this version contains no redactions, it is five pages shorter than another declassified version.

each report that led to his "extraterrestrial" hypothesis. Hence the contradiction, either the sightings were not evaluated, or they were. In the same paragraph, the Panel contradicts itself on this point.

About the potential of the threat, the Panel stated that it agreed with the assessment of the CIA Office of Scientific Intelligence. There was no direct threat. But related dangers included:

> "a. Misidentification of actual enemy artifacts by defense personnel.
>
> b. Overloading of emergency reporting channels with 'false' information (noise to signal ratio analogy – Berkner).
>
> c. Subjectivity of public to mass hysteria and greater vulnerability to possible enemy psychological warfare."

The two concerns requiring the need to intervene in the public arena are (b) & (c). The concern over false flying saucer reports clogging emergency communications was a short-term worry at best. The psychological warfare concerns were based in social science but were recommended by physical scientists. It was a recommended action developed by the CIA Office of Scientific Intelligence and probably the CIA Psychological Review Board. To date, there are no declassified documents about the relationship between the Robertson Panel and the CIA's Psychological Review Board. Both (b) & (c), above, are about developing the means to control the public and eliminate its fascination with flying saucers.

These "indirect" threats were the first substantive matter presented to the panel. The CIA staffer who presented the "indirect" threat analysis was Marine Officer Philip Strong. His recommendation, at the start of the proceedings, was to quash the public's interest in flying saucers, thereby eliminating UFOs from public discussion. To deal with the issue of public gullibility, the Panel-recommended alternative was public education. However, the Air Force/CIA wanted to reduce public discussion of flying saucers. The "Comments and Suggestions" recommended a two-pronged approach, training and debunking. The training program, developed independently by the Panel, was never implemented. Follow-up efforts concentrated on the limitations of public discussion of flying saucers. The "debunking" recommendation became the standard response from the federal government for decades. This course of action was later considered an impediment to our understanding of this phenomenon by the Office of the Director of National Intelligence in the Navy's UAP Task Force June 25, 2021, *Preliminary Assessment*. The "debunking" or "stigma" policy is, by today's admission, still interfering with our understanding of the phenomenon.

CHAPTER TEN

PANEL REPORT DISTRIBUTION

Going into the Panel, the Air Force and CIA set the table to serve up their recommendations. After the July 1952 Washington, D.C. flap, President Truman publicly called for a fresh look at the phenomenon. In response, Air Force and CIA personnel determined what needed to be done was not a fresh look, but a way to tamp down interest in the phenomenon. With their recommendations approved by the Robertson Panel, the Air Force and CIA got what they wanted. While they quickly ignored the Panel's suggested public education component, other aspects were selectively circulated throughout the administration.

The Air Force, after thinking that the flying saucer era was ending, saw a spike in 1952. A growing percentage of the public believed in the extraterrestrial hypothesis and not the Air Force explanation. If the summer of 1953 saw a similar spike in sightings, it would cause a loss of faith in the Air Force's ability to defend our airspace. While flying saucers did not ever rise anywhere near level of concern of the Soviet Red Scare, flying saucers were gaining traction as a public policy topic. The newly formed Air Force was riding a wave of negative publicity, being unable to answer basic questions about the UFO phenomenon. The Air Force needed flying saucers out of the public's mind.

The CIA had similar concerns. It claimed flying saucers were a source of manipulation by the Soviet Union. The CIA wanted to both deny the Soviets this weapon; while developing UFO-like sightings to confuse the enemy and gain a tactical advantage. Considering that intelligence reports showed no Soviet mention of flying saucers in its state-controlled media, use of this type of psychological warfare was not possible. Since the spy agency had no practical ability to use flying saucers as a psychological weapon behind the Iron Curtain, the real purpose was to use this weapon against Americans, violating the CIA "no internal security function" prohibition.

After the Panel finished its work, the CIA acted quickly. On January 21, 1953, the CIA Office of Scientific Intelligence prepared a memo to the file detailing the results of the Robertson Panel's deliberations. The memo's "fair statement of the conclusions reached" is as follows:

> "1. No evidence is available to indicate any physical threat to the security of the United States.
>
> 2. No evidence is available to indicate the existence or use of any as yet unknown (to us) fundamental scientific principles.
>
> 3. The subject 'UFO' is not of direct intelligence interest. It is of indirect intelligence interest only insofar as any knowledge about the innumerable unsolved mysteries of the universe are of intelligence interest.
>
> 4. The subject 'UFO' is of operational interest for three reasons:
>
> (a) Interference with air defense by intentional enemy jamming or lack of ability on the part of operating personnel to discriminate between radar anomalies and actual airborne weapons.
>
> (b) Related to (a), interference with air defense by overloading communication lines from the air defense observation stations.
>
> (c) Possibility of a psychological offensive by the enemy timed with respect to an actual attack could

conceivably seriously reduce the defense effort of the general public."[116]

As to the first two conclusions, the memo mirrored established U.S. government policy. First, there was no physical threat to the United States and, second, nothing in these reported sightings was beyond 1953 scientific boundaries.

The third conclusion talks about indirect intelligence interest in one of the "innumerable unsolved mysteries of the universe." This conclusion conflicts with the second conclusion that "(n)o evidence is available to indicate the existence or use of any as yet unknown (to us) fundamental scientific principles." However, the key finding needed to reassure public officials and the public was that the UFO phenomenon was not a threat. If you combine the second and third findings, it is not a threat to the United States, even though we may not understand it.

From a civil liberties perspective, the fourth conclusion was of more concern. The UFO phenomenon (a) is a threat because of military radar issues; (b) may be the cause of panicked calls that mask an attack; and (c) could be used for psychological warfare against the U.S. However, there is little discussion of radar interference (4(a)) in the Robertson Panel Report. Better radar would more quickly fix the problem of "instant identification" of hostile forces. Any "public education" program would take years to change public attitudes. Within four years, the radar identification problem would be fixed with the completion of the DEW radar line. The "debunking" strategy was intended to solve a longer term "problem," public interest in UFOs.

The conclusions found in 4(b) and 4(c) specifically addressed this long-term problem. As discussed earlier, there was only

---

[116] Memorandum to File, Meeting of OSI Advisory Group on UFO, January 21, 1953, DOC_0005515967.

speculation about psychological effects, first by Air Force and CIA staff in late 1952. The Panel echoed these concerns based on the draft report prepared by CIA staff and Lloyd Berkner, who did not attend most sessions. The declassified record shows scant evidence to justify the recommendation. The input and recommendations of the CIA Psychological Review Board are still classified. Their declassification could provide some answers. Did the board provide counsel about the implications of a domestic psychological warfare campaign? Perhaps, the AARO could shed light on their influence in domestic policies intended to manipulate the American public.

On January 30, 1953, the CIA Office of National Estimates (ONE) held a briefing about the findings of the Robertson Panel.[117] In attendance were a retired admiral, a retired ambassador, and Dr. Edgar Hoover. Presumably, Dr. Hoover was FBI Director J. Edgar Hoover since the FBI was to be kept informed about UFO developments. ONE was tasked with developing intelligence estimates for the IC. Currently, that task is handled by its successor, National Intelligence Council under the Director of National Intelligence. Besides receiving a copy of the report, little is known about the ONE briefing.

After the ONE briefing, news of the classified Panel Report was circulated throughout the CIA and eventually to interested agencies in the executive branch. On February 6, 1953, the CIA bureau chiefs were sent a memo describing the recommendations of the Panel.[118] In contrast to the file memo of January 21, 1953, discussed above, the February 6 memorandum used language directly from the Panel Report on the need to take active measures to delegitimize flying saucers and those who report them. This memo sent a clear signal throughout the CIA that the threat

---

[117] Briefing ONE Board on Unidentified Flying Objects, January 30, 1953, Doc. 0000015353.

[118] Bureau Chiefs, February 6, 1953, DOC 0005515969.

centered on domestic discussion of UFOs rather than the possible reality of the phenomenon.

After internal circulation, CIA Director Allen Dulles sent copies to Secretary of Defense Charles Erwin Lewis, Director of the Federal Civil Defense Administration Val Peterson, and Chair Jack Gorrie of the National Security Resources Board at the White House.[119] Dulles states that the primary responsibility for the subject does not lie with the CIA. Yet, the Agency continued to be involved according to declassified documents. The Air Force remained in the lead role in investigating the phenomenon, while the CIA monitored the phenomenon, but focused on the people who investigated it.

The report was sent to newly installed members of the Eisenhower Administration. None of the recipients had the foreknowledge or the capability to contest the recommendations. Jack Gorrie had recently joined the national security staff at the White House from state government. Secretary of Defense Charles Erwin Wilson had just come from the private sector (General Motors) and would be unaware of the issue. Civil Defense Director Val Peterson had been on the job for a couple of days when he received the report. Even though his agency was directly affected by the policy recommendations, Civil Defense was not involved in the formulation of the Robertson Panel recommendations. In the FCDA annual reports of 1952 and 1953, there is no mention of a concern for the problem of panic from a Soviet "false flag" UFO invasion. If this were a serious concern, the civil defense authorities would be the appropriate agency to address the problem, especially for the Panel-recommended public education efforts.

The Panel concluded that the UFO phenomenon could be used to confuse or hamper civil defense. However, the civilian agency

---

[119] *i.e.,* Letter to Secretary of Defense Charles Erwin Lewis, March 13, 1953, CIA Doc 01676R001000160043-9.

responsible (FCDA) was never part of the policy formulation process. None of its plans or procedures were discussed. Its aircraft identification training program for civilian observers was never raised. Without FCDA participation, the findings regarding preparedness for a Soviet air attack amounted to guesswork. In the 1953 FCDA annual report, the subject of warning the public of an impending nuclear attack was discussed:

> "Warning Time
>
> It is assumed that civil defense officials will receive some warning of an impending air attack. Although complete surprise is possible, it is assumed that approximately 15 minutes' warning can now be given to the public. More warning time will be given to the public if it is available. As the installation of radar nets and other detection measures progresses, the possibility of complete surprise will decrease.
>
> It will never disappear entirely, however, and no one can ever guarantee all parts of the United States against surprise attack. Surprise is most likely to be achieved in an attack by guided missiles launched from submarines."[120]

The 1953 annual report discusses the installation of "radar nets and other detection measures" just before DEW Line across Canada and Alaska began construction in 1954. The most likely surprise came from non-nuclear guided missiles, fired from submarines.[121] Assuming the Soviets had the capability at the time, the missiles would not be mistaken for flying saucers, given the flight

---

[120] Federal Civil Defense Administration 1953 Annual Report, p. 11; https://www.hsdl.org/c/abstract/?docid=34712.

[121] At the time, nuclear devices were not small enough to be placed on submarine-launched missiles. Nuclear weapons were delivered by aircraft, coming over the polar route from Russia.

characteristics and short flight duration that early sub-based missiles had from launch to landing.

This 1953 FDCA report does talk about the possibility of panic, but not from the source discussed by the Robertson Panel. Instead, the annual report draws upon the recent wartime experiences instead of speculation:

> "The surest antidotes to panic are knowledge, training, and leadership.
>
> Knowledge of what the danger is. Knowledge of what to do about it to the point where the proper reaction is instinctive. Knowledge that something is being done about it, by people who know their business. Knowledge of what is happening, and why right after it happens. Knowledge that the Nation's leaders are on the job by seeing and hearing them on television and radio.
>
> This attack on potential panic was perhaps the most important single mission of FCDA's public education program in 1953. It embraced both individual and family pre-attack indoctrination and training, and blueprints for specific measures in the attack and post-attack phases designed to allay fear, combat rumor, and restore confidence and the will to win."[122]

Even after having the benefit of the Robertson Panel Report, federal civil defense authorities did not incorporate any of the Robertson Panel's threat assessments into their public education efforts. Panic was an issue, but not from flying saucer reports. Civil defense authorities were worried about the public knowing how to prepare for an imminent attack and making sure that public

---

[122] Federal Civil Defense Administration, 1953 Annual Report, p. 67; https://www.hsdl.org/c/abstract/?docid=34712.

officials would be able to reassure the public that the proper steps were being taken. One can tell from the tone of the statement, FCDA relied upon the trust people had in government at the time. A far cry from today's skepticism.

The Robertson Panel Report makes a short reference in the comments by Panel members about the 1938 *War of the Worlds* Mercury Radio broadcast. The psychology of the civilian population during previous attacks, such as Pearl Harbor, would have shed more light on how the public would react to an attack. Rather than evaluating evidence on the impact of actual events, the Robertson Panel relied upon a conclusion reached by the Air Force and CIA staffs developed months before the Panel proceedings.[123] These conclusions were based on speculation that did not impress the FCDA.

Declassified records show the CIA was concerned about the impact of future UFO sightings. Several follow-up CIA memos talk about the concern that there may be another increase in sightings in the summer of 1953 following the summer 1952 wave. The CIA was leaving the investigatory role to the Air Force. However, the CIA Office of Scientific Intelligence did keep watch on UFOs "in view of possibly greater activity this summer" (1953). Declassified documents showed that the CIA's role was to clandestinely reduce the amount of information about the small percentage of cases that could not be explained.

When issued, the Robertson Panel Report, in the eyes of many, led to a new "dark ages" of UFO investigation, where the Air Force abandoned even the pretense of scientific effort. While the Air Force continued to retain astronomer, Dr. J. Allen Hynek, explanations of serious cases sometimes became farcical. Dr. James

---

[123] Flying saucers, September 11, 1952, DOC 0000015343.

E. McDonald, professor of astrophysics (University of Arizona), commented upon this shift as follows:

> "As nearly as I can tell, the January 1953, Robertson Panel Report marked the turning point with its regrettable decision to leave the UFO problem in the hands of a group not primarily concerned with scientific matters, and at the same time to have them shift to debunking policies to decrease public interest in the entire matter. It remains a very puzzling period, and an extremely important one in the history of UFO studies."[124]

It took years for the Air Force to make the Robertson Panel Report available. The intervention of a congressional committee was required. While the CIA released differing "sanitized" versions over the years, one thing is apparent. The study's recommendations went beyond a "scientific" review and made recommendations that had significant domestic civil liberties implications.

As stated by University of Arizona professor, Dr. James E. McDonald, the Robertson Panel Report marked a sea change in the way people were treated who advocated an extraterrestrial hypothesis. While the Air Force had issued reports with similar conclusions about the nature of the phenomenon, the Robertson Panel Report gave license to discriminatory treatment of groups and individuals who had witnessed or advocated the reality of the phenomenon. By the end of 1953, the Air Force issued a companion policy that required civilian pilots to report every UFO sighting to the Air Force, bypassing civilian air travel regulators. After the Air Force and CIA policies were initiated, reports from witnesses with trained observational skills began to dry up. The public reports made by trained professionals became "professional suicide" for

---

[124] National Investigations Committee on Aerial Phenomenon, *United States Air Force Projects Grudge and Bluebook Reports 1–12*, Forward @ p. ix, Washington, D.C. (1968).)

those brave enough to still step forward. Any public witnesses that reported what they saw to military or civilian authorities had their views misrepresented and, if they presented compelling physical evidence, it would be taken, kept, or returned in an altered state.

In the aftermath of the CIA panel's report, the Air Force conducted a briefing in Los Angeles with the major commercial air carriers. At the briefing, the UFO reporting process was explained. Airline industry attendees were cautioned not to allow their pilots to publicly discuss their UFO sightings.

The rationale for the Robertson Panel to recommend steps for stifling speech was clothed behind worries of the "communist menace," The early 1950s were a time when all national policy questions were seen through the "communist threat" prism. Civil liberties were restrained with the justification of protecting us from communism. With belief in a possible Soviet attack masked by a mass hysteria/UFO incident, the Robertson Panel felt restrictions on the conduct of flying saucer advocates were both necessary and appropriate.

The UFO "problem" came at a difficult time for America. The flying saucer era was ushered in during the beginning of the Cold War with its civilization-ending nuclear stakes. Between 1947 and 1953, the foundation for a 40 plus year struggle for global supremacy was laid. The struggle was more than just a military confrontation. It was a battle between ideologies, authoritarianism (communism) versus democracy. This post-World War II challenge for supremacy lasted until the collapse of the Soviet Union. However, during this initial phase, the outcome was very much in doubt.

UFOs were a wild card added to this global struggle. The possibility that another, superior technological civilization might take an active role in deciding our future was a great challenge by itself. Whether the source of this new phenomenon was from our planet or not, resources needed to be redirected from the Cold War to face this new challenge. Squelching efforts to study the phenomenon would give the military time to figure out a response.

The new challenge put another layer on the existing U.S.-Soviet struggle with an unknown force of unknown origin and unknown intentions. The consensus of the military and intelligence communities felt this mysterious force had to be dealt with without creating panic. As in other trying times, the rights of a few were affected for what was thought to be the greater good. Congress was kept out of the loop. In other words, normal democratic methods were sidelined.

The arrival of the modern flying saucer era came while the Air Force and CIA were still trying to establish their own internal policies. The Air Force and the newly reconstituted Department of Defense were created in the summer of 1947, just as the country was buzzing about Kenneth Arnold and the beginning of the flying saucer era. As the mystery took on new meaning in 1952, the Central Intelligence Agency was called in by President Truman to help deal with this new problem. With the help of a scientific panel that could reassure members of the Eisenhower Administration, the Air Force and CIA formed a partnership that would shape the way the phenomenon was viewed by the public. At the same time, the issue was isolated from congressional involvement. The newly created CIA and Air Force developed policies that would never survive normal legislative oversight today.

CHAPTER ELEVEN

THE CIA IMPLEMENTS DEBUNKING

Having ignored the only independent recommendation calling for a "public education" program, the CIA moved to "debunk" saucer reports through clandestine means. Numerous memos talk about the CIA's need to keep its involvement secret from the public. This secrecy was both pre- and post-Robertson Panel. Prior to the Panel, the CIA and Air Force quietly met and formulated a strategy that led to the bulk of the Robertson Panel recommendations. Afterwards, the CIA began implementing the recommendation where "the national security agencies (would) take immediate steps to strip the UFOs of the special status they have been given and the aura of mystery they have unfortunately acquired."

The distribution of the Panel's recommendations was during the first two months of the Eisenhower Administration. The three senior level players who received a copy of the bare bone's recommendations were Secretary of Defense Charles Erwin Lewis, Director of the Federal Civil Defense Administration Val Peterson, and Chair Jack Gorrie of the National Security Resources Board. All came recently from outside of government and none were in a position to contest the recommendations from CIA Director Allen Dulles, the brother of Eisenhower's Secretary of State, John Foster Dulles. While the new Federal Civil Defense Administration director responded by requesting a meeting on the recommendations, there is no record, even though one was scheduled, that any FCDA/CIA meeting on this subject ever took place.[125]

The CIA and Air Force took full advantage of the transition between administrations. CIA Director Allen Dulles had been the assistant director in the Truman Administration, so he was in a senior management position throughout the process. Dulles's position under the Truman CIA gave him access to the thinking and policy opportunities "the problem" presented to the soon to be unleashed intelligence community. The change in administrations brought about a change at the CIA that emphasized clandestine operations. Under the Eisenhower Administration, the "problem" remained in Air Force and CIA hands. No follow-up directive was issued by the White House as originally contemplated. The CIA wanted the "problem" handled informally, as one memo stated, without a lot of delaying paperwork. Paperwork is how you document policy. The policy was not made publicly available.

Besides distribution of the report, the CIA began active measures to implement its recommendations. On February 6, 1953, the CIA distributed a memo to all its bureau chiefs about the Robertson Panel recommendations. The memo discussed the basic conclusions including the recommendation "(t)hat the national security agencies take immediate steps to strip the Objects of their special status they have been given and the aura of mystery they have acquired."[126]

---

[125] Further to FDCA Meeting, April 24, 1953, DOC 0000015360.

[126] Bureau Chiefs, February 6, 1953, DOC 0005515969.

Three days after the memo to bureau chiefs, the FBI[127] reported a contact with one of the scientists who was a member of the Civilian Saucer Investigators-Los Angeles. CSI-LA was one of the two organizations that the Robertson Panel said must be "watched."[128] The FBI memo was only sent to the Office of Scientific Intelligence (assistant for operations) regarding the "California Committee for Saucer Investigations" (*sic*). The memo talked about an interview with Dr. Walther Riedel, a guided missile project engineer at North American Aviation Corp. The opening paragraph stated:

> "1. Recently, a member of the Los Angeles Office had occasion to hear Dr. Walther Riedel tell something of the activities of the California Committee for Saucer Investigation (CSI). His comments, as follows, may be of interest."

This opening comment portrays this meeting as pure happenstance. Within days after every CIA bureau received a memo pointing out the recommendations to "watch" CSI-Los Angeles and "strip" flying saucers of their "special status," an FBI agent meets with a CSI member who held a security clearance, and a contact memo was written to the CIA Office of Scientific Intelligence.

This CSI member was not ordinary. Dr. Walther Riedel was a German rocket scientist who helped design the German V-2

---

[127] This memo was probably written by an FBI agent, while detailed to the Los Angeles FBI Field Office. The Robertson Panel Report had not been formally distributed outside of the CIA at this point. However, "Dr. Edgar Hoover" had attended the CIA ONE briefing on January 30, 1953. This must have been a reference to FBI Director J. Edgar Hoover. However, the contact memo is not in the FBI archives, but it is in the CIA archives. There is no separate record of Hoover formally receiving a copy of the Panel Report even though the FBI was to be kept apprised of UFO developments. Hoover must have authorized the contact after learning about the Panel's recommendations at the ONE briefing.

[128] California Committee for Saucer Investigation, February 9, 1953, CIA-RDP81R00560R000100030023-4.

rocket.[129] He came to America as part of Operation Paperclip, a program that brought former Nazi scientists to the U.S. after World War II. Based on the timing and tenor of the interview, it is hard to believe that the meeting/interview was an accident.

Dr. Riedel was one of several North American Aviation Corp. employees who were members of CSI-LA. CSI-Los Angeles was a small, volunteer organization that brought science to the investigation of UFOs. It had been mentioned in a *Life Magazine* article about flying saucers and the subsequent notoriety led to CSI-LA receiving a flood of sighting reports from around the world. Its expertise was also written about in *Time Magazine*, *Reader's Digest*, and numerous newspapers. CSI-LA produced a small newsletter listing sightings it had investigated. Its budget was modest, and its work was done by volunteers.

The FBI contact memo mentioned another North American scientist, George P. Sutton, who was also a member of CSI. The memo states that Sutton spoke to the American Rocket Society in December 1952 about Soviet rocket development. The memo concludes with the following:

> "Of incidental interest may be the fact that NAA (National Aeronautical Association) suggested politely and perhaps indirectly to Dr. Riedel that he disassociate himself from official membership on CSI."

The interview with Riedel implements the Panel recommendation of "stripping" the UFO problem of one of its most

---

[129] http://astronautix.com/r/riedelwalther.html. This short biographical note about Dr. Riedel claims, in part, that the contact was concerning whether he was a Nazi. However, the memo does not discuss the loyalty issue. It discusses his association with CSI-LA. Since Riedel came to the U.S. in the CIA Operation Paperclip program, the government would already know about his Nazi party membership. Being a party member was a requirement to be in the German rocket program.

qualified observers. The bottom line after Dr. Riedel was visited by a federal agent and subsequently left CSI-LA. Within a year, the CSI organization lost active members with security clearances and went out of business.

Since other North American Aircraft employees were CSI-LA members, the visit received by Dr. Riedel must have had a chilling effect on other CSI-LA members who did defense work. The CIA picked on the most high profile and vulnerable member of CSI-LA. Riedel was brought to the United States by the U.S. government under the Operation Paperclip program. A visit from a government agent with inquiries about outside activities would not be seen as a benign contact. It furthered the goals of the Robertson Panel to eliminate the threat of qualified outside experts investigating UFOs.[130]

The fact that a prominent scientist whom the government brought to America to work on critical defense projects was approached by a government agent would make any CSI-LA member question their involvement. It could cost them their security clearance. The overall environment of the period would make anyone concerned about such contacts. This period was also known as the "Red Scare" with ongoing investigations of anyone who might not be "loyal" to the United States. The House of Representatives Committee on Un-American Activities was holding hearings in Los Angeles during this same time, interviewing famous "reds" such as comedian Lucille Ball. This atmosphere surely contributed to the concern that was felt by defense workers who, in their spare time, studied something that was subject to official ridicule.

_____

[130] A good source for many of the documents about this period and CSI-LA information can be found at the website, Project 1947: Sign Historical Group. http://project1947.com/shg/.

The contact memo's tone is informal to the point of being whimsical. The contact agent had the "occasion" to visit with Riedel and discuss his UFO activities. The FBI contact memo claims the National Aeronautical Association had stated "politely and perhaps indirectly to Dr. Riedel that he disassociate himself from official membership on CSI." The contact memo was written in a way that shows that Riedel was under pressure from an alleged outside source to remove himself from flying saucer investigations. It reads as if the FBI or CIA had no role in the scientist ceasing to study UFOs.

This "contact" so close in time to the ONE briefing of the Robertson Panel recommendations is an unlikely coincidence. First, what was the legal authority for an FBI agent to contact Dr. Riedel about a private activity? Even with the contact made by the FBI, it was initiated by the CIA. The CIA had no legal ability to investigate matters inside the boundaries of the United States. The contact was an "internal-security function" prohibited by law. The FBI held exclusive authority to conduct counterintelligence operations in the United States. This contact was made at the request of the CIA, and it received the memo three days after it was written.

As today, background checks on security clearances were the exclusive province of the FBI. However, the contact was not part of a background check. Hence the odd tone of the February 9, 1953 memo. It would have been a violation of law for the CIA to investigate an employee of an American company on American soil. The contact memo reads as if the source of this information was a person who had knowledge of the overture to Dr. Riedel, but not the exact method. The language that "perhaps indirectly" would indicate that the contact agent got his information from another source. It was not routed through the FBI. It went directly from the FBI agent to the CIA bureau in charge of UFO issues.

This approach to Dr. Riedel was about a private activity shared by many at the time. Based on other declassified documents, it wasn't the only action taken to strip UFO study of its "aura." By the end of 1953, declassified records indicate that the CIA's focus was not on investigating UFOs but on trying to tamp down public discussion of the "problem." This is borne out in a status memo drafted on December 17, 1953, by Todos M. Odarenko, chief of the Physics and Electronics Division of the CIA Office of Scientific Intelligence.[131] The memo talks about the drop in sightings between 1952 and 1953 and discusses the efforts of the various branches of the military. In a redacted part of the status report, it mentions the UFO investigation efforts by the CIA in foreign nations. In 2010, when this report was declassified, the survey of foreign nation efforts in the UFO field was still classified. The final paragraph of the status memo discusses the impacts of the recommendations by the Robertson Panel. It states as follows:

> "Results of OSI Panel Recommendations. The consultants who considered this problem in January 1953 recommended that UFOB's be stripped of special status and aura of mystery and that policies on intelligence, training and public education pertinent to true indications of hostile intent or action be prepared. The definite drop in the number of "sightings" reported in 1953 over 1952 **could be attributed to actions following these recommendations**. Two recent books ('Flying Saucers From Outer Space' by Keyhoe and 'Flying Saucers Have Landed' by Leslie and Adamski) take full advantage of 'official' UFOB reports released by the Air Force to develop a central theme that UFOB's are extraterrestrial in origin. Fortunately, the later book is so nonsensical and obviously fraudulent that it may actually help calm down public reaction.

---

[131] Current Status of Unidentified Flying Object (UFOB) Project, DOC 0005515979.

These books do, however, illustrate the risk taken by the present policy. There are no other as yet apparent results of these recommendations."[132] (*emphasis added.*)

Almost a year after the Robertson Panel Report was circulated around the executive branch, the focus was still on the people and private groups that discuss UFOs. Eliminating the "problem" from public debate was the central theme of the status report. The memo tries to take credit for the drop in sightings that are "attributed to actions following the recommendations." Since no educational program was ever started by the Federal Civil Defense Administration or the Civilian Aeronautics Authority (forerunner to the Federal Aviation Administration (FAA)), it is difficult to see what "actions" were taken to reduce the number of 1953 sightings. The only remaining implementation measure was "debunking" or stigmatizing UFO advocacy. The December 1953 status report refers to "actions" taken. Only one action taken is found in the currently declassified records. It is the visit to Dr. Riedel to discuss his private activities studying UFO sightings. The question is what other 1953 "actions" were taken to strip UFOs of their special status among the American people? Throughout this period, the declassified CIA memos discuss the lack of necessity for documentation of Agency UFO efforts. Is this based on bureaucratic inefficiency or an effort to hide actions taken to discourage domestic free speech about UFOs and their possible origin?

Today, the AARO and the Comptroller General have the ability to review the classified record to see other steps taken to implement the Robertson Panel recommendations. Records of the Physics and Electronics Division of the CIA Office of Scientific Intelligence would be a good place to start. Are there other contact memos about

---

[132] Ibid.

private study of UFOs? After 1953, it is clear from the public record that the number of pilots, scientists, and other trained observers who reported UFOs dropped. Media outlets lost their best private sources of information about the phenomenon. Qualified sources of information began to dry up, leaving the Air Force narrative essentially unchallenged. It could continue to "debunk" sightings without having to answer difficult questions raised by trained observers. As will be shown, the CIA efforts complimented Air Force policies that depressed public information from quality observers in the wake of the Robertson Panel recommendations.

CHAPTER TWELVE

THE CAT IS OUT OF THE BAG

In 1956, Edward Ruppelt published a book about his Project Blue Book experiences. Capt. Ruppelt had participated in the Robertson Panel proceedings and disclosed the existence of the secret report.[133] The book was vague about its contents. Ruppelt did not mention its CIA sponsorship or the names of Panel members. Later, a heavily redacted version was released after a 1958 records request from Dr. Leon Davidson of the National Investigations Committee on Aerial Phenomenon (NICAP), a UFO research group. However, NICAP wanted the full, unredacted copy of the report. Prior to any response, a meeting was held to discuss possible release of the Robertson Panel Report.[134]

Dr. Davidson was, according to the memo of the meeting, "quite insistent" about getting a full copy. In addition to Air Force and CIA Office of Scientific Intelligence personnel, a representative of the CIA Legislative Counsel's Office[135] was present. The assembled group determined to withhold the full report. The reasoning was that paragraph 3 of the report "cites examples that could be taken by an enemy with possibly dangerous consequences to national

---

[133] Ruppelt, Edward J., *The Report on Unidentified Flying Objects*, (Original 1956 Edition) Doubleday & Company (1956), reissued Cosimo Classics (2011), pp. 190, 211–215.

[134] Meeting with Air Force Personnel Concerning Advisory Scientific Panel Concerning Unidentified Flying Objects, dated 17 January 1953, May 16, 1958. DOC 005516044. (Declassified in 2010.)

[135] The CIA's Legislative Counsel was the liaison to Congress.

security." The full report was not released and has yet to be released to this day. The group also discussed their contacts with Robertson Panel members. None had any problem with having their names released, but none wanted to have it known that they had any connection with the CIA.

The concern in the Robertson Panel recommendations was more about its political impact than the stated defense concern. It reads as follows:

"3. The Panel further concludes:

a. That the continued emphasis on the reporting of these phenomenon does, in these parlous times, result in a threat to the orderly functioning of the protective organs of the body politic.

We cite as examples the clogging of channels of communication by irrelevant reports, the danger of being led by continued false alarms to ignore real indications of hostile action, and the cultivation of a morbid national psychology in which skillful hostile propaganda could induce hysterical behavior and harmful distrust of duty constituted authority."

At the time, the concern over mass hysteria "clogging" phone lines was without merit. By July 15, 1957, the DEW radar line extended from Vancouver Island to across the Arctic. The Air Force had a fully operational early warning system that made the need to rely on citizen observers obsolete. No enemy could use the Robertson Panel Report to learn about any vulnerabilities since the construction of the DEW radar line was complete, and not a secret.

The real concern was the language about how UFOs had cultivated a "morbid national psychology" which could induce "hysterical behavior and harmful distrust of duty constituted authority." These proclivities were aimed at the American people. Tying the CIA to these "dangers" would open a door to inquiry about its motives. The fact that the CIA had been clandestinely involved in the domestic aspects of UFO interest would raise red flags in Congress and could provide a ready campaign issue to the Democrats in the upcoming 1958 midterms.

The timing of the May 16, 1958 meeting was particularly concerning. It was just months before the congressional August recess when Congress hit the campaign trail. 1958 was the last congressional midterm before the end of the Eisenhower Administration. A scandal about CIA involvement in a domestic issue could become a campaign advantage to the benefit of Democrats. After Republicans gained majorities in the House and Senate in 1952, Democrats regained both legislative houses in 1954 and increased their hold on Congress in 1956. Heading into the 1958 midterms, which usually work against the President's party, the last thing CIA legislative counsel wanted to do was open up the Eisenhower Administration to scrutiny over a secret CIA report that assumed the American people were subject to manipulation because of their supposed "hysterical behavior." Since NICAP was calling for congressional hearings, the timing could not have been worse for the CIA.

The assembled group determined to issue an Air Force press release about the Robertson Panel. It was thought that the issuance of the release would forestall future public inquiries. Legislative counsel felt that this approach would help deal with congressional concerns and the legislative counsel's office representative, George Cary, would review the press release for the CIA. The memo's main concern was keeping public interest at a minimum.

The Panel's recommendations about how to control the UFO debate were founded on speculative theories of "mass hysteria" or the creation of a "morbid national psychology." Scientists who designed radar, nuclear weapons, bombsights, and other weapons of war were asked to recommend drastic measures that gave license to unconstitutional conduct. None had any training or special knowledge in mass psychology. Despite their prestigious pedigrees, they were not trained to render legal or psychological opinions. The Air Force and CIA used a distinguished group of patriotic scientists to justify civil liberty violations against a small, but potentially influential, group of Americans. However, the public was unaware of the rationale used to support these speech restrictions on private activity. Keeping knowledge about the secret Robertson Panel was in the best interests of the CIA and Air Force.

Apart from participating in the Robertson Panel, the Air Force did its part to implement the Robertson Panel's recommendations. The Air Force, as part of the defense department, helped put together a joint protocol to identify and report unusual activity in the sky. A joint Army, Navy, Air Force protocol (JANAP-146) was issued in December 1953.[136] This joint protocol was based on an Air Force regulation 200-2 that was adopted in August 1953. The policy prevented public disclosure of reports. JANAP-146 governed military and civilian pilots. It required reporting of different classes of objects as follows:

> "201: INFORMATION TO BE REPORTED AND WHEN TO REPORT
>
> a. Sightings within the scope of this chapter, as outlined in Article 102b(1), (2), (6) and (7), are to be reported as follows:
>
> (1) While airborne (except over foreign territory – see paragraph 2102. and from land-based observers.
>
> (a) Single aircraft or formations of aircraft **which appear to be directed against the United States** or Canada or their forces.
>
> (b) Missiles.

---

[136] https://www.nsa.gov/Portals/70/documents/news-features/declassified-documents/ufo/janap_146.pdf

(c) **Unidentified flying objects**.

(d) Hostile or unidentified submarines.

(e) **Hostile or unidentified** group or groups of military surface vessels.

(f) Individual surface vessels, submarines, or aircraft of **unconventional design, or engaged in suspicious activity** or observed in an unusual location or following an unusual course.

(g) Unlisted airfields or facilities, weather stations, or air navigation aids.

(h) Any unexplained or unusual activity which may indicate a possible attack against or through Canada or the United States, including the presence of any unidentified or other suspicious ground parties in the Polar region or other remote or sparsely populated areas." (*emphasis added.*)

Unidentified flying objects are a category separate from aircraft, missiles, or seagoing vessels. By its terms, the reporting requirements are applicable to all military pilots and "US and Canadian civil and commercial aircraft." (JANAP- 146, §102(b)(1).) It was a crime for a private pilot to fail to report a UFO. (JANAP-146, §208.)

The term "unidentified flying object" is listed as a separate category than airplanes, ships, or submarines. UFO subsection 201(a)(1)(c) contains language that does not limit the type of unidentified flying objects that must be reported. All UFOs must be reported. "UFO" was an Air Force term in general usage at the time. The other categories talk about unidentified aircraft, submarines, or surface ships. The categories used in JANAP-146 §201 separate these different types of manufactured objects. A basic rule of regulatory legal construction is that subjects separated into different categories are intended to be defined as being separate and distinct. UFOs are different from all other object categories.

Regardless of the appropriate legal interpretation, pilots at the time thought that the regulation criminalized discussion of UFOs. JANAP-146 put commercial pilots in a dilemma. If they reported a UFO, it could threaten their status as a commercial pilot. Publicly discussing a report made under this regulation would be a crime as a disclosure of the contents of a "report." (JANAP-146, §208.) Whether or not they could be prosecuted, commercial pilots *thought* they were at risk of prosecution if they violated JANAP-146.

In early 1954, the Air Force held a meeting with representatives of commercial airlines. At this meeting, the requirements of the Air Force policy were discussed. The Scripps-Howard News Service published two articles about the meetings. It was reported that the airlines were warned not to allow their flight personnel to publicly discuss UFO sightings.[137]

In response, a New Jersey newspaper started a national petition to overturn the Air Force regulation. A December 22, 1958 article in the *Newark Star-Ledger* discussed a petition by 50 commercial pilots protesting the punitive measures about failure to report or publicly discuss a UFO sighting. Each could subject the commercial pilot to jail time or a $10,000.00 fine.[138] Each of the 50 pilots had seen a UFO while in flight. Eventually, over 400 pilots signed the petition. Despite these protests, the restrictions remained in effect.

A commercial pilot who reports a UFO through the JANAP-146 process would have a follow-up interview with Air Force

---

[137] A Scripps-Howard News Service report of February 13, 1954 stated, in part, that: "Airline pilots are asked not to discuss their sightings publicly or give them to newspapers." http://project1947.com/fig/1954a.htm.

[138] https://www.theufochronicles.com/2016/01/airline-pilots-protest-us-government.html.

intelligence personnel. If they do not report under JANAP-146 and talk to a reporter, the failure to report to the Air Force would create problems for them and their airline. A review of news stories from the period shows a decline in commercial pilot reports after 1953. The flying saucer era started with a pilot reporting nine UFOs. Some of the best reports of UFOs came from commercial pilots pre-1953. The July 24, 1948 report by two Eastern Airlines pilots who were on landing approach near Montgomery, Alabama was one of the best documented UFO reports. The fact that the pilots encountered an unknown object in restricted airspace was a credible threat to the safety of their passengers, regardless of what federal policy stated. Most pilots stopped reporting UFOs and stopped commenting to the press and public. The Air Force had criminalized free speech by commercial pilots of their sightings of UFOs if they talked to the press about a sighting.

The inclusion of UFOs in the list of "must report" objects had a "chilling" effect on pilots. They could not talk to the press because the attendant publicity would raise the question of whether or not they officially reported. If they reported through official channels, they would be told not to speak of it publicly. No matter which way they would talk about a sighting, officially or publicly, both their airline and their own flight status would be put in jeopardy. Therefore, including UFOs in the types of phenomenon that should be reported had a significant impact on the free speech rights of pilots. Because of the concern about UFOs interfering with commercial aircraft and no place to have a report taken seriously, the National Aviation Reporting Center on Anomalous Phenomenon (NARCAP) was founded in 2000 to accept anonymous pilot reports.[139]

The UFO reporting requirements helped the Air Force eliminate some headaches it had knocking down pilot reports. The

---

[139] http://www.narcap.org/.

Air Force needed to lower public concern and focus its attention on threats it could handle. Keeping experts like pilots from speaking out left the Air Force as the only authoritative UFO experts. In fact, one of the most qualified experts at this time worked for the CIA, photo interpretive legend Arthur C. Lundahl. While working at the Naval Photo Interpretation Laboratory in 1952, Lundahl reviewed the Tremonton footage and vouched for its authenticity after retiring. [140]

> "These were indeed UFOs. The film showed objects of unknown size moving at high speeds—one of our estimates was 1,700 miles an hour—and they were changing colors from reds to blues to greens and back to reds.... Obviously, moving at 1,700 miles per hour in 1952, it couldn't have been an aircraft—either on line or in research by any government. We had access to that data and knew it could not have been that. And we had experts determine that it was not the reflection of any light source or any heavenly body."[141]

Lundahl did not change his opinion about the Tremonton film. As the chief photo interpreter for the CIA, he was in charge of upgrading their capabilities from the propeller aircraft era to the space age. After retirement, he still believed that the July 1952 film showed true UFOs.

While the Robertson Panel recommendations that all UFOs could be explained is subject to debate, the "debunking" and surveillance recommendations are not. The Air Force

---

[140] Hall, Michael David and Conners, Wendy Ann, *Captain Edward J. Ruppelt: Summer of the Saucers-1952*, Rose Press International (2000), pp. 132–133. *See generally*, Swords, Michael and Powell, Robert, *UFOs and Government: A Historical Inquiry*, Anomalist Books (2012), pp. 170–203 (Chapter Nine: "*The CIA Solution*").

[141] Hall, Michael David and Conners, Wendy Ann, *Captain Edward J. Ruppelt: Summer of the Saucers-1952*, Rose Press International (2000), p. 133.

implementation of the UFO reporting requirements also raises serious civil liberty concerns. Official policy was that UFOs were not a threat to national security, so a regulation requiring mandatory reporting by civil and commercial pilots could not be based on national security concerns. The Air Force was not the agency in charge of civilian and commercial aviation. The CAA, the forerunner of the FAA, played that role. Regulatory intervention by the Air Force was not justified.

As will be discussed, other serious legal and constitutional concerns arise from the Robertson Panel recommendations. Such as recommending that government intelligence agencies "watch" non-violent civilian organizations and discourage free speech rights of U.S. citizens. None of their recommendations appear to have been vetted by any legal counsel. Later involvement of CIA legislative counsel was for the purpose of getting stories straight between the Air Force and the CIA over how to keep information out of congressional hands. Transparency about the Robertson Panel's work was the last thing these officials wanted. CIA/Air Force needed to cover up their actions before, during, and after the Robertson Panel.

CHAPTER THIRTEEN

FREEDOM OF ASSOCIATION

The first known consequence of the Robertson Panel recommendations was a visit by a federal agent with Dr. Walther Riedel.[142] The memo documenting the visit was written only eight days after the first internal briefing about the Robertson Panel recommendations. A briefing that included FBI Director J. Edgar Hoover. The FBI contact of Riedel occurred three weeks after the final report was submitted and before it was circulated to outside agencies. To this day, the name of the contact agent is still redacted and only the CIA Office of Scientific Intelligence apparently received a copy.

The agent talked to Dr. Riedel about his association with CSI-LA. The private organization was one of the two cited by the Robertson Panel as a threat that needed to be "watched." Dr. Riedel was part of CSI-LA's investigation team for UFO sightings. It was a private activity where the scientist was part of a team that was curious about UFOs. The agent discussed the impact private flying saucer research would have on Dr. Riedel's professional standing.

While people have a right to engage in private activities, the fact they are being questioned by a federal agent about their personal life is unnerving. Any reasonable person would seriously consider disassociating themselves from CSI-LA so as not to "make waves." The fact that a federal agent was inquiring about the group would raise alarm bells to any CSI-LA member with a security clearance.

---

[142] California Committee on Saucer Investigation, March 9, 1953, CIA-RDP81R00560R000100030023-4.

Thanks to *Life Magazine* and other prominent news sources, CSI-LA was known around the world. They had volunteer scientists and engineers who applied science to their UFO studies. However, with a declining rank of volunteer investigators, CSI-LA closed up shop by 1954. The Air Force and CIA were worried about a repeat performance of the 1952 flying saucer wave in summer 1953. This required quick action. If there was another wave in 1953, groups like CSI-LA could be credible sources to contradict Air Force explanations.

The visit to Dr. Riedel was the first known action to implement the Robertson Panel recommendations that can be gleaned from declassified documents. A later CIA memo (December 1953) indicates it was not the last. This single visit by a government agent to the right person shows how small steps can have large results. At the time, there were very few groups that were studying the UFO phenomenon. Only two were mentioned in the Robertson Panel Report, CSI-LA, and the Aerial Phenomenon Research Organization (APRO). APRO was started by a couple from Wisconsin (James and Coral Lorenzen). It was the first group to gain a nationwide membership. While it did not have the same kind of scientific depth as CSI-LA, it was beginning to gain a foothold by linking up flying saucer clubs around the country. Founded at the beginning of 1952, it was present for the 1952 wave. If the Air Force and CIA were concerned about another wave, APRO was also poised to be a key player in the public's mind.

Both CSI-LA and APRO had newsletters that went out to members. Pre-internet newsletters let small groups of people who share a common interest keep up with developments. APRO's newsletter tied small groups around the country together. Being the local representative of APRO gave local news outlets a ready source for information about the phenomenon that often contradicted official explanations. Of the two organizations, CSI-LA had the most highly trained members who were taken seriously by news media, such as *Time Magazine*. If you were going to "strip" flying saucers of the "aura" they had "unfortunately" acquired, CSI-LA, with its technical/scientific depth, would be a good place to start.

Under the Constitution's First Amendment, free speech is guaranteed to citizens, including their right to "associate" with others. While the term "freedom of association" is not found in the First Amendment, courts have interpreted the First Amendment to include the right of citizens to gather together and discuss common interests. It has been expressed as follows:

> "The exercise of those textual freedoms presumes the availability of opportunities for human dialogue and united action, without which the expressly provided rights would be meaningless. The right of association thus ensures individuals the freedom to choose with whom, and what causes they will gather to exercise First Amendment freedoms."[143]

One cannot exercise free speech rights without sharing your ideas with others. This associational right is held by every citizen and allows them to choose the groups and individuals they wish to associate with to discuss ideas of their own choosing. While there are a few limits, i.e. "inciting imminent lawlessness," the popularity of the idea is not important. In fact, courts offer protection to groups that hold unpopular or controversial ideas.[144] The government cannot put up barriers to private group membership based on either the "viewpoint" of the speaker or the subject matter "content" discussed.

Freedom of association is one of our most fundamental rights. Interference with this "expressive activity" (speech or conduct meant to express an idea) must:

---

[143] Ides & May, *Constitutional Law: Individual Rights* Sixth Ed. (2013) Wolters Kluwer, p. 440.

[144] *Roth v. U.S.* (1957) 354 U.S. 476.

"...be justified by regulations adopted to serve **compelling state interests, unrelated to the suppression of ideas**, that cannot be achieved through means significantly less restrictive of associational freedoms."[145] (*emphasis added.*)

The government is required to have a "compelling" interest that is not related to the suppression of ideas. It must be implemented by the least restrictive means that have a negligible impact on fundamental speech or associational rights.

When you break down the reasoning behind the Robertson Panel's recommended need to "debunk" UFO study, the reason is because of the "mass hysteria" that a fake UFO incident would cause. Yet the record shows no testimony by experts in group psychology or any expertise in group behavior. Physicists have no more expertise in mass psychology than any other college graduate who took first year psychology. Experts are used to making recommendations in fields where they have superior knowledge. If the subject is outside of their expertise, they are not experts. The Robertson Panel had no experts in mass psychology yet recommended restricting the speech of people holding contrary views to official government policy.

The Panel also did not study the extent of defensive measures employed by the Air Force. Specifically, there was no study of the defense measures in place to alert the military that an attack was imminent. The Federal Civil Defense Administration was never part of this process, even though it was the agency in charge of civilian preparedness. FCDA never listed this fake UFO theory as a concern in any of its public reports. No compelling governmental interest was shown that the UFO "problem" would interfere with the ability

---

[145] *Roberts v. United States Jaycees* (1984) 468 U.S. 609, 623.

of the military to respond to a sneak air attack by Soviet propeller-driven bombers.

The Air Force had a civilian Ground Observer Corps from 1952 to 1958. There is no record of any involvement of this group with the Robertson Panel proceedings. There is no record that the Corps was ever informed of the recommendations of the Panel. Since it was the Ground Observer Corps that called in their reports of a possible enemy air attack to the Air Force, their involvement would be crucial if the "jamming" of phone lines were of concern. Also, any public education program, as recommended by the Robertson Panel, would involve this civilian observer group.

None of these possible avenues was investigated. The CIA panel went directly to the "debunking" and surveillance. The Robertson Panel went to the most speech-restrictive option first, even though less restrictive options were available. In other words, there was no "compelling governmental interest" to restrict speech when other reasonable means were available.

These rights of free speech and freedom of association are the foundation of our democracy. The CIA and Air Force determined before the Panel was formed that the "real" concern with UFOs was the people who talk about them and join in groups to study them. The Panel of experts chosen, and the evidence presented, do not legally justify the conclusions reached about "debunking" and surveillance. While each scientist on the Panel had contributed mightily to protecting the United States, the CIA and Air Force used their scientific stature to justify unconstitutional restrictions on the public.

The Robertson Panel recommendation to "strip" UFOs of their "aura" and a "morbid" fascination by the public shows that the Panel and its CIA and Air Force sponsors were targeting people for discussing UFOs. Stopping talk about UFOs was a main goal of the Panel recommendations.

The Robertson Panel recommendations to "strip" UFOs of their "aura" through "debunking" also fails on the final part of the test, requiring the least restrictive means used to implement a valid governmental purpose. The surveillance of specified groups and the "debunking" of ideas are not the least restrictive means of preserving military readiness. The concern was that the Soviets would launch fake UFOs over United States territory and panicked citizens would clog military phone lines and prevent people from calling in to alert the Air Force of an actual attack.

First, did the Air Force rely on phone calls from the public to alert it to a sneak attack? No, it did not. From 1952 to 1958, only trained civilian observers were part of the process. In addition, the Air Force had radar and air patrols with trained personnel assigned to be able to distinguish friend from foe. While its early warning radar line was still in the construction phase, the early warning DEW Line was mostly over Canada and Alaska. Flights from the Soviet Union over the Arctic would fly for hours over unpopulated areas outside of the continental United States. Restricting information about flying saucers would not solve the need for "instant identification of unknown objects."

Second, public telephone lines were not used by military personnel to communicate with each other about a possible Soviet attack. The Ground Observer Corps had phone lines to the Air Force that were not available to the public. The military used radio communications on secured channels that allowed communications with advanced units such as patrol planes. The Air Force also had signals intelligence operations that would intercept Soviet radio messages. The Soviets controlled attack aircraft with ground-based commands. Since the North Koreans used the same tactics, the Korean War gave the Air Force a lot of knowledge about the Soviet's heavy reliance on radio communication with its aircraft. Robertson Panel member Lloyd Berkner was one of the government's experts in radio communications. He had been an assistant for Vannevar Bush on the defense committee that controlled weapons development so he would have known classified information about the state of signals intelligence.

Even assuming that public telephone lines were used for pre-attack communications, there were other alternatives that would not restrict civil liberties. The Air Force could add more phone lines. They could establish dedicated phone lines to local civil defense, law enforcement, or other trusted sources of information. They could also follow the Robertson Panel's single recommendation developed solely by the Panel. They could advocate to the White House an educational program on flying object identification for the public.

Any of these options are preferable to an attack on the expressive conduct of the public. People who hold the view that UFOs are worthy of study are entitled to associate with like-minded people without government interference. Regardless of the accuracy of their opinions, they are protected by the freedom of assembly privilege under the First Amendment.

The CIA used a government agent's conduct to put a wedge between CSI-LA and its membership. This fledgling private organization lost its most important members during 1953. The ones who had the credentials to study the objects being seen around the world. Without the credibility of these scientists and engineers, CSI-LA was just another flying saucer club made up of untrained people who could convince themselves but few others. To use a term used by the CIA, CSI-LA was reduced to a group of "saucer buffs" who had no technical expertise. Any advocacy of a policy requiring the government to publicly study UFOs would be severely hampered because of this brain drain precipitated by government interference.

This situation is a classic example of why the First Amendment guards against discrimination based on what organizations citizens are allowed to join. Without the ability to seek out others who have a common interest, other First Amendment freedoms would be extremely limited. The United States Supreme Court has spoken out on this issue in many cases, but the most prominent case is *NAACP v. Alabama*.[146] During the civil rights struggles of the 1950s, the State of Alabama tried to prevent the NAACP from doing business in Alabama. As part of their efforts, they subpoenaed the membership list of the civil rights organization. The Supreme Court held that the request was a violation of the NAACP and its members' constitutional rights. When speaking about the freedom citizens have to assemble without government interference, the Supreme Court stated as follows:

> "It is hardly a novel perception that compelled disclosure of affiliation with groups engaged in advocacy may constitute as effective a restraint on freedom of association as the forms of governmental action in the cases above were thought likely to produce upon the particular constitutional rights there involved.... Inviolability of privacy in group association may in many circumstances be indispensable to preservation of freedom of association, particularly where a group espouses dissident beliefs."[147]

In *NAACP v. Alabama*, the issue was confidential membership lists. Since many members of CSI-LA worked in the defense industry, the leverage of a security clearance allowed the government to interfere with the ties between key members and their organization. The Supreme Court noted that the protection extended even to groups with "dissident beliefs." Here, we have an organization that holds dissident beliefs. These Americans believed that flying saucers warranted serious study.

---

[146] *National Association for the Advancement of Colored People v. Alabama* (1958) 357 U.S. 449.

[147] Ibid. @ p. 462.

The timing and tenor of the federal agent's approach to a vulnerable individual shows the intent was to discourage people with technical expertise from investigating UFOs in their spare time. The recently declassified records show how quickly the CIA acted on the Panel recommendations. Since the goal of the CIA was to "keep paperwork to a minimum," we are left to ponder how many other instances that the CIA interfered with people's constitutional right to freely associate with other persons who wished to study this taboo subject.

CHAPTER FOURTEEN

PRIOR RESTRAINT OF SPEECH

At the end of 1953, a CIA status report on the UFO issue was sent up the chain of command to Assistant Director for Scientific Intelligence Marshall Chadwell.[148] It was an assessment of the success of the Robertson Panel's recommendations. Written by Todos M. Odarenko, Chief of the Physics and Electronics Division of the CIA Office of Scientific Intelligence, the year-end report commented on the 1952 publication of two books on UFOs. "These books do, however, illustrate the risk taken by the present policy."

The "risk" of the CIA policy of "debunking" was that it was not strong enough to prevent the publication of UFO books. This statement helps explain the mindset of the CIA and Air Force at the time. They had decided certain private speech should be prohibited. Usually, the press speaks out against this type of censorship. In this case, most in the press felt the same way about UFO coverage as the CIA/Air Force. It was not deserving of constitutional protection.

Coincidently, in 1953, the CIA began a program that paid journalists for their help. Some were recruited to be the eyes and ears of the Agency overseas. But others were based in the United States, including some of the most important journalists in the country. There were at least 400 journalists that were on the CIA payroll during this period.[149] Having journalists paid to help the

---

[148] https://www.cia.gov/library/readingroom/docs/DOC_0005515979.pdf.

[149] Bernstein, Carl, "The CIA and the Media," *Rolling Stone Magazine*, October 20, 1977, pp. 55–67. The reporter who helped break the Watergate story details how the CIA ran a domestic program to influence coverage through 1973

CIA get its message out could be one of the "actions" taken according to the year-end 1953 report.

Did journalists help the CIA with its UFO "debunking" policy? The journalists did not need much detail to be of assistance. An "off the record" explanation that a classified panel of scientists recommended UFOs be debunked to prevent mass panic during a Soviet attack would be a sufficient explanation to secure their assistance. It is reasonable to assume that journalists helped to implement the "debunking" policy, whether they knew the details of the "debunking" policy or not.

The two books mentioned in the 1953 memo were on opposite ends of the UFO spectrum. One book, *The Flying Saucer Conspiracy*, was by a former Marine aviator, Donald Keyhoe. It was his second book on the subject. His first, *Flying Saucers Are Real*, sold half a million copies. Psychologist Carl Jung considered his two books on UFOs to be free from "wild speculation."[150] The commentary by Jung shows the global reach of the Keyhoe books. It also highlights the efforts of many in the budding UFO community that took a sobering, fact-based approach to the subject.

The other book was co-authored by George Adamski. He was a "contactee" or a person who claimed to have regular visits from space people. In his case, it was a beautiful woman from Venus. The CIA's status memo's assessment of Adamski's tale is probably accurate. The Adamski book made some pretty bizarre, uncorroborated claims. However, as we know from today's headlines, even people making bizarre claims are protected by the First Amendment. It is easy to see why the comments in the memo about a book claiming visits by beautiful space women might work

---

by major U.S. media outlets. The article also explains how the CIA was able to keep this program out of the report of the Church Committee.

[150] Jung, Carl, *Flying Saucers: A Modern Myth of Things Seen in the Skies*, p. xiii, (1961).

to the advantage of the CIA narrative. Accurate or not, stories like Adamski's helped with the "debunking" policy. As opposed to Keyhoe's book, the average reader might look unfavorably upon Adamski's claims.

The final sentence of the status report laments that following the Robertson Panel recommendations did not prevent the publication of two books about UFOs. This is a stunning statement. It means that the implementation of the "policy" was intended to stop people from publishing books about UFOs. The worldwide distribution of Keyhoe's book gave him a large platform to raise serious questions about the U.S. government's UFO policy. Taking this status report at face value raises serious questions about what other steps the CIA took to lower public interest in the flying saucer "problem."

The 1953 status memo questions whether the CIA was doing enough. It questions whether more should be done to stop future books. Yet, writing a book is a form of speech. An author engages in expressive conduct when they write. Both of Keyhoe's books raise questions about Air Force policy. The First Amendment's free speech clause protects citizens' rights to publish their ideas without government interference. The "actions" taken by the CIA in 1953 failed to achieve their goal, which, in part, was intended to curtail interest in the phenomenon. Serious study of the UFO phenomenon would contradict government policy and, in the words of the Robertson Panel, would be "a threat … to the body politic."

Preventing a book from being published stops speech before it happens. It is a "prior restraint" in that it stops expressive conduct before it occurs. A book that questions government policy is protected speech unless it advocates violence or uses classified information that the author illegally obtained. Keyhoe did neither. His books do not advocate violence and were based on public information. This year-end 1953 memo indicates an intent to suppress the publication of information about a subject that the government finds uncomfortable. However, the Constitution's free speech clause was intended to protect the right to disagree with government policy.[151] The United States Supreme Court has enunciated some strict standards to prevent government from interfering with speech, especially before it is uttered or written. In the famous *Pentagon Papers Case*,[152] the Court stated that:

> "Any system of prior restraints of expression comes to this Court bearing a heavy presumption against its constitutional validity."[153]

Even a subject involving national security does not allow suppression of government criticism. In the *Pentagon Papers Case*, the U.S. Supreme Court held that exceptions to free speech protections for national security purposes are meant to be narrowly limited. Since 1931, the Supreme Court has stated that it will presume that the prior restraint is invalid absent significant information to justify the interference with speech rights.[154] To overcome the heavy presumption of illegality in the *Pentagon Papers Case*, U.S. Supreme Court Justice Brennan stated that the government must show a court proof "that publication must inevitably, directly, and immediately cause the occurrence of an event of required gravity" to justify preventing the publication. Even though classified materials in the *Pentagon Papers Case* were received by the *New York Times* and *Washington Post*, the newspapers did not illegally remove them or aid

---

[151] *Roth v. U.S.*, 354 U.S. 476 (1957).

[152] This case was about the publication of classified information detailing unfavorable information about the conduct of the Viet Nam war. It was leaked by a whistleblower, Daniel Ellsberg, from the Pentagon. The *New York Times* and the *Washington Post* published excerpts and the Nixon Administration unsuccessfully sued to stop publication.

[153] *New York Times Co. v. United States* (1971) 403 U.S. 713, 714.

[154] *Near v. Minnesota* (1931) 283 U.S. 687.

in their unauthorized removal.[155] This strict standard requires the government to have strong reasons and no other alternative to prevent a newspaper from publishing information of interest to the public.

As applied to this circumstance, the government would have to prove that the publication of a UFO book would "immediately" cause the harm the government was worried about. In other words, the CIA or Air Force would have to prove in court that a UFO book would create panic or some other harm as soon as it was published. For instance, the government can prevent the publication of information about how to build a nuclear bomb, which could immediately lead to the creation of weapons of mass destruction.[156] However, the government cannot stop publication of a book based on arguments of hypothetical future harm.

Here, the CIA status memo highlighted the dilemma the CIA and Air Force had in trying to "strip" flying saucers of their "aura." Declaring that UFOs are not real does not give the government the right to impede persons from arguing a contrary viewpoint. Similarly, the government cannot stop people from talking about a subject because of unproven "mass hysteria" claims. Public knowledge of this policy would highlight its unconstitutionality. "Debunking" amounted to suppression of speech the government disagreed with and wanted stopped.

Even if one of the books (*Flying Saucers Have Landed* by Leslie and Adamski) was completely false, the government does not have the right to prevent its publication. The government is not an arbitrator of the truth in a public debate.[157] Even if all UFOs are from a

---

[155] *New York Times Co. v. United States* (1971) 403 U.S. 713, 727.

[156] i.e. Atomic Energy Act of 1954, 44 United States Code § 2011 et. seq.

[157] *United States v. Alvarez* (2012) 567 U.S. 709.

terrestrial source, the publication of a book advocating a different position is constitutionally protected.

Coupled with the efforts to stop scientists and engineers from investigating UFO sightings as part of an organized group, like CSI-LA, made 1953 a bellwether year for CIA and Air Force efforts to "debunk" UFOs. Even though the Robertson Panel recommendations never became a national security directive, declassified documents now show that the CIA/Air Force implemented the bulk of its policies in a way that violated the civil rights of many who wished to discuss UFOs.

The CIA's later claims its reluctance to acknowledge its involvement was to protect itself from embarrassment. However, declassified records show that one of the CIA's motivation was, in large part, to cover up unconstitutional acts against American citizens. These constitutional violations were part of the policy's foundation. A policy that was intended to eliminate a "threat to the orderly functioning of the protective organs of the body politic."

As will be shown, the Air Force and CIA policies to restrict discussion of UFOs went beyond the 1953 efforts. Many of these efforts can be seen from declassified records and extend to this day. They may explain today's reluctance of the Air Force and the CIA to assist Congress in its study of UAP.

CHAPTER FIFTEEN

EVERY PICTURE TELLS A STORY

Today, any picture too good to be true is likely "photoshopped." In the 1950s and 60s, it was more difficult for people to alter photographs. Photographic images were a big part of magazines during that time. Almost every coffee table in American living rooms had magazines that occasionally showed pictures of flying saucers. *Look* and *Life Magazines* had high circulations. Each ran stories about flying saucers. Some of these stories included pictures that allowed each American to judge for themselves. Any government attempt to "strip" UFOs of their "aura" would have to limit the number of quality UFO photographs in the public domain. Both the Air Force and the CIA conducted efforts to keep photos and other documentary evidence out of the public domain.

What emerged became a familiar story. First of all, most quality UFO photos were taken by people who showed little or no prior interest in flying saucers. The photographer just happened to be in the right place at the right time. The 1950s-60s photographers used cameras that were not available to the average person before the war. The post-World War II period also saw a proliferation of 8 and 16-millimeter handheld movie cameras. Still photography was also available to people of modest means. Most American families had portable cameras using Kodak film. Some used Polaroid cameras that developed within minutes. People documented vacations, picnics, birthday parties, and other family events. Mass production brought photographic equipment into nearly every home in America. It was not surprising that some amateur photographers captured images of flying saucers.

Most photos of UFOs, then as now, were indistinct objects that had a simple explanation, such as a reflection of light. However, a small number of these photos showed structured objects at close range that were difficult to dismiss. A smaller number of "home movies" showed unexplainable images of strange objects in motion. In this era, a familiar pattern emerged for hard to explain home movies and photographs.

In the case of the two movies reviewed by the Robertson Panel (Tremonton/Warrant Officer Delbert Newhouse & Great Falls/Nick Mariana), the footage was taken by experienced photographers of moving objects. Neither set out to capture a flying saucer on film. Most photos were taken in the company of corroborating witnesses, usually family.

Except for Polaroid cameras, the film would be sent to the local drugstore or mailed to Kodak for development. A single set of pictures and negatives would be returned to the photographer after commercial processing. Once returned, they would be shown to family and friends. The photographer who captured an unknown object would become the focus of local attention whether they wanted notoriety or not. For example, Nick Mariana, a minor league baseball executive whose film was reviewed by the Robertson Panel, showed his film to service clubs around Great Falls. All would marvel at these curiosities and gossip about the photos would spread. When local media would learn of the film, the flying saucer mystery would have a "local angle." The photographer would often be asked to speak on local radio, grant permission for the local newspaper to publish them, or they would appear on local television. The photographer and witnesses would become minor celebrities, many unwillingly.

Even people who did not want to be bothered would become known as the person with the flying saucer photo. As with all neighborhood secrets, gossip quickly spreads the word. Eventually, the unique photograph would become known to the media and the

Air Force would learn of the footage. As mentioned earlier, Project Blue Book had a newspaper clipping service to supply them with UFO news accounts from around the country.

Once the Air Force learned about the photos, they would send officers from its Office of Special Investigations (AFOSI) to the home of the photographer. The agents would request to look at the original photos and negatives. Being a time of trust in government, witnesses routinely turned over their film to official looking men carrying government IDs. Most of the witnesses who took photos were not interested in flying saucers until they saw one. They trusted a government that would later ridicule their sighting and destroy key evidence that substantiated their account.

Both photographers who filmed the UFOs seen by the Robertson Panel claim that their films were altered before their return. The segments removed contained the best views of the UFOs. The Montana minor league baseball executive had shown his film around town at service clubs. As a result, he had many credible witnesses who had seen the unspoiled version of his film. Mr. Mariana confirmed that the original film had close shots of two spinning disks that were removed from the footage when the remaining portion was returned to him.[158] Of the 315 frames of film, 35 frames were removed by the Air Force.[159] Later, the Air Force borrowed the remaining footage from baseball executive Nick Mariana after the Air Force agreed to sign a "no edit" agreement.[160]

The other film reviewed by the Panel was also alleged to have been altered in Air Force custody. The Tremonton, Utah film was

---

[158] Clark, Jerome, *The UFO Book: Encyclopedia of the Extraterrestrial*, Visible Ink Press (1998), pp. 397–401.

[159] Stringfield, Leonard, "inside Saucer Post ... 3-0 Blue: CRIFO Views the Status Quo: A Summary Report" The Moeller Printing Co. (1957), p. 71.

[160] Clark, Jerome, *The UFO Book: Encyclopedia of the Extraterrestrial*, Visible Ink Press (1998), pp. 397–401.

taken by a naval photographer, Warrant Officer D.C. Newhouse.[161] He had been transferred to the West Coast and was driving his family to Oregon when he took the movies. The current public version shows multiple glowing objects at a distance. Delbert Newhouse stated that the Air Force removed "frames" of the movie showing a single UFO moving away over the horizon. The redacted portions would have provided some ranging information and help determine the object's location and speed. This portion of the "home movie" was missing when the film was returned.[162] Famed CIA photo analyst Arthur Lundahl, who saw the Newhouse film while a naval civilian employee, stated: "I've seen a genuine film of UFOs that, as a photo analyst, I believe could not have been faked."[163]

Another well-documented incident involved the FBI and the Air Force trading charges about a missing photograph. On February 21, 1960, at approximately 1:00 A.M., an amateur astronomer, while taking pictures of the Moon, took a 35mm picture of an object that puzzled him. Joseph Perry of Grand Blanc, Michigan was using his homemade telescope at a setting of 350–400 power to photograph the Moon. After developing the film, he noticed one of the slides showed a circular object, silhouetted by the Moon, with a dome on top. Having no real knowledge of UFOs, he did not know what he had captured on film. After showing the slide to several customers at his pizza restaurant, he agreed with his customers' assessment and concluded that he captured a photograph of a classic flying saucer. On March 5, 1960, Perry contacted the local FBI field office to ask for assistance in getting his picture to the proper authorities.

---

[161] https://www.ufocasebook.com/tremontonutah.html.

[162] Ibid.

[163] https://www.theufochronicles.com/2017/06/cia-photo-analyst-authenticates-ufo-film.html.

According to an FBI report, Perry took 20 color photos of the Moon through his telescope.[164] Only two of the photos were not under exposed. One of the clear photos showed the Moon. According to declassified FBI files, the other photo "he observed what appears to be a flying object somewhere between the end of his telescope and the surface of the moon." The object was flat on the bottom, oval shaped, appeared to have a fluorescent glow around it, and was moving as it had a vapor trail running behind it.

He furnished both color slides[165] to the FBI. On March 9, 1960, a cover memo was sent, along with a news article from the *Detroit Times* to FBI Director J. Edgar Hoover about Joseph Perry's photos. The cover memo mentions that the two photos were sent to the Air Force 25th District Office AFOSI at Selfridge Air Force Base in Mt. Clemens, Michigan. The cover memo stated that: "(t)he Air Force was requested to return the slides to Mr. Perry."

The FBI field office sent a teletype on the afternoon of the same day to Director Hoover. It mentions that the local FBI office corrected the *Detroit Times* article when it stated that the FBI was investigating the matter. The FBI policy, since September 1947, was to not conduct any investigations of flying saucers. All investigations were supposed to be handled by the Air Force. The Air Force was supposed to keep the FBI apprised of developments to help the FBI perform its law enforcement and counterintelligence responsibilities. However, declassified records show that the FBI maintained an interest in the subject and the people who were involved in the study of the phenomenon.

---

[164] https://vault.fbi.gov/UFO/UFO%20Part%2014%20of%2016/view (Part 14 of 16). The FBI records on this matter are mixed with other UFO-related issues from the same time period.

[165] "Slides" were small pictures that fit into a slide projector that would project the image onto a large screen.

After the local publicity, Joseph Perry was contacted by the National Investigations Committee on Aerial Phenomenon (NICAP) and other UFO organizations. Each told Perry that he would never get his photographs back. As a result, Mr. Perry wrote a letter to President Eisenhower. He mentioned the NICAP and other UFO "societies" advisories. In the March 21st letter, Perry asked the President to make sure he got his photos back.[166]

On March 26th, the White House referred the letter to FBI Director Hoover for handling. The FBI received the letter to the President on March 29th. A quick turnaround for a letter sent to the White House from Michigan eight days prior. The day before FBI Director Hoover's receipt of the White House correspondence, the special agent in charge of the Detroit field office sent the Director a status report. This report details the motivation of Mr. Perry behind his White House correspondence and explains that the local FBI office had communicated updates about the situation to the Air Force intelligence office that received the photos.

On March 28, 1960, the FBI field office sent Director Hoover an article about Joseph Perry in the *Flint Journal*, which made clear that the FBI had forwarded the two photos, and the work of the local FBI agents was concluded. The memo quotes Perry saying: "The only way I will be satisfied if I don't get it back is if the Government tells me it is top secret." The status report concludes by stating that the Selfridge Air Force Base Office of Special Investigations was advised on all issues discussed in this memo.

On April 6th, FBI Director Hoover took it upon himself to communicate directly with AFOSI at Selfridge Air Force Base. He pointed out the FBI policy to refrain from investigating UFO sightings. The correspondence also attached a copy of Mr. Perry's letter to the President. In the FBI files, there is no response from the

---

[166] https://vault.fbi.gov/UFO/UFO%20Part%2014%20of%2016/view (**Part 14 of 16**).

Air Force and there are no declassified records about this matter in the Air Force archive. Later, on April 12th, FBI agents from the Detroit field office visited Joseph Perry to explain that the FBI does not investigate UFOs. He was told the local FBI office turned over his photos to the Air Force and he should seek redress from the Air Force. According to the memo to the FBI director, Mr. Perry was satisfied with the FBI's handling of the matter and expressed his "appreciation" to them.

On April 21, 1960, Director J. Edgar Hoover wrote to Mr. Perry, stating:

> "I am in receipt of your letter dated April 13, 1960, and I wanted you to know that I have taken the liberty of furnishing the Department of Air Force with a copy of your letter so that agency could reply to you concerning the return of the photographs you furnished to Special Agents of this Bureau. As you have been previously advised, these photographs, when received from you, were immediately furnished to the Office of Special Investigations, Department of the Air Force, Selfridge Air Force Base, Mount Clemens, Michigan.
>
> It is suggested that you direct further inquiries in this matter to the Department of the Air Force."[167]

Mr. Perry never got his photos back. He was never told that the photos were "top secret." There is no information in the Air Force files that contradicts the FBI memos. If the Air Force never received the photos, the FBI memos to Washington would not be accurate. Either the Air Force is covering up what it did with the photographs, or the FBI field office was lying to Director J. Edgar Hoover.

---

[167] Ibid.

The Air Force confiscation and/or tampering with Joseph Perry's UFO photo fits a familiar pattern. The photographer was not interested in flying saucers prior to the taking of the photos. He felt it was important that government authorities review the unique evidence. Trust in government was at a high point in post-World War II America. Because of his trust in the government, he didn't make a copy prior to turning over his evidence. He, like the two photographers of the movies shown to the Robertson Panel, did not get back his film in original condition.

The *modus apparandi* of the Air Force is consistent in these examples and many others, including one documented later in Chapter Seventeen. A photographer with no prior interest in UFOs would document an unexplainable event. Friends, customers and/or relatives would marvel at the unknown object. One of the people given access would pass along a tip to the media. The press would arrive and make the photographer a minor celebrity, whether they wanted it or not. The Air Force's Project Blue Book subscribed to a news clipping service which would gather news stories on UFOs. These services would literally "clip" the story out of the paper and send it to the client.

The local Air Force base would send AFOSI intelligence officers to the home of the photographer. After chatting with the photographer about the sighting, the officers would ask to take the original photos and negatives with them for analysis. Assurances would be given that the film would be returned when the Air Force had finished with them. Unless the photographer inquired, they would never hear from the Air Force again. Often times, the Air Force would claim the photos were hoaxed by the person who voluntarily gave up the originals.

It is important to note that any confiscation of private property by the federal government amounts to a "property taking without compensation" and violates the Fifth Amendment of the United

States Constitution.[168] In *Horne v. Department of Agriculture*, Chief Justice John Roberts recently restated that private property, like photographs, receive the same protection against seizure as real property (land). Since England's *Magna Carta*, common law protections have been in place, prohibiting the government from taking property without due process of law. In each of the examples, the Air Force took the property without paying reasonable compensation and without a legal process where the photographer could contest the "taking." In addition to the value of the photographs, the person who owned them would usually have their reputation damaged by the action when the Air Force claimed that the photos were hoaxes.

In each example, none of the photographers were involved with any UFO organization prior to taking their pictures. Through no fault of their own, they were thrust into the spotlight as the "guy" who took the flying saucer picture. For being a loyal American that cooperated with the Air Force, each would be without a defense against any official effort to discredit them as a "flying saucer nut" or for perpetrating an outright fraud. The more they claimed that they had been wronged by the government, the more they would be viewed as suspect by the average person who trusted the government. Nick Mariana, who took the Great Falls, Montana film, quietly disappeared from his baseball executive position after the incident. Without evidence, it is hard to defend yourself in the media or from Air Force allegations.

The handling of the Joseph Perry photos is particularly instructive. He turned his photos over to the FBI. The Federal Bureau of Investigation spent significant effort to distance itself from the Air Force conduct. These efforts included a personal letter from J. Edgar Hoover, the long-time FBI director, steering Mr. Perry towards the Air Force with his legitimate grievance. The

---

[168] See, *Horne v. Department of Agriculture* 135 S. Ct. 2419 (2015).

correspondence located in the FBI archives show that the Air Force was aware of the FBI's efforts to explain that they merely were a conduit of the photos. None of the official correspondence contains any reference from the Air Force that they failed to receive the photos from the FBI. Much later, that became their story. It was only after Mr. Perry was told by every UFO organization that contacted him that the Air Force would never give back the photos. People who did not closely follow the UFO phenomenon would be unaware of the Air Force's retention/destruction policy.

While Director Hoover stated that the FBI did not investigate flying saucers, declassified records tell a different story. Hoover had authorized the use of FBI personnel to attend UFO meetings and report back. For example, in 1960, while Mr. Perry's drama was playing out, Hoover received a four-page, single-spaced account of a UFO meeting in Denver, Colorado.[169] The meeting's main speaker talked of his views about UFOs and their intentions. Nothing discussed at the meeting was of law enforcement interest. No mention is made of any threats of violence, threats to overthrow the government, or of any ties to a hostile foreign country. Despite the lack of any legitimate law enforcement interest, the report was sent only to Director Hoover. Undoubtedly, some people tried to take advantage of the flying saucer craze to make a quick buck. However, there was no apparent reason for an FBI agent to attend this particular meeting and send a memo only to Director J. Edgar Hoover.

Throughout the FBI UFO archives, there are many letters to citizens which explain that the FBI does not investigate UFOs. However, like the CIA, the FBI monitored UFO groups. J. Edgar

---

[169] https://vault.fbi.gov/UFO/UFO%20Part%2014%20of%2016/view (Part 14 of 16). The FBI records on this matter are mixed with other UFO-related issues from the time period.

Hoover was keeping tabs on non-violent citizens merely because they believed in a fringe subject.

Also, these instances are not the only ones where the FBI investigated controversial groups based on their particular viewpoint.[170] Hoover was likely the first non-CIA official to be informed about the results of the Robertson Panel while attending the CIA ONE briefing on January 30, 1953. Within days of the briefing, an FBI agent documented a meeting with a prominent member of CSI-LA, dissuading him from pursuing UFO study.

Overall, the efforts of the Air Force to take credible evidence out of the public domain raise serious questions. Were they trying to restrain speech that they disagreed with? Were they damaging peoples' reputations merely because they wanted to "keep a lid" on UFOs as a subject of public policy debate? As discussed in the previous chapter, the government cannot restrain speech because it does not agree with it.

Today, there is no need for the Air Force to misappropriate photographs. All that is needed is to claim that the photographic evidence has been "photoshopped." It is likely that most photos of UFOs on the internet today have been altered or created. Technology has done the Air Force's job. Today, people do not trust photographic evidence. Today, there is hardly a sighting that comes to light without an internet search result that starts with the label "hoax." The official government policy has been that all sightings are misidentifications, delusions, or outright hoaxes. While that policy has been called into question today, this policy appears to

---

[170] https://www.npr.org/2012/02/14/146862081/the-history-of-the-fbis-secret-enemies-list; Church Committee (U.S. Senate Select Committee on Intelligence Activities Within the United States), *Intelligence Activities and the Rights of Americans: 1976 U.S. Senate Report on Illegal Wiretaps and Domestic Spying by the FBI, CIA and NSA*, Red and Black Publishers (2007).

still be a guiding public policy. The question becomes: What actions are still being taken to keep the genie in the bottle?

CHAPTER SIXTEEN

NOW YOU SEE IT, NOW YOU DON'T

The last chapter showed examples of how the Air Force used deceptive means to reduce the amount of high quality evidence available to the public. They used loyalty to the country against its own citizens to obtain and destroy evidence. It furthered the policy goal intended to "strip UFOs of their aura they have unfortunately acquired." Today, technological advances raise a different problem. With the explosion of data, sometimes publicly available documents show more than the government wants known. When documents inadvertently show too much about UAP, they disappear from government websites under suspicious circumstances. The examples used herein show how quickly the government reacts to discovery of UFO/UAP evidence. Like early tactics to get rid of extraordinary photos, the goal is to suppress quality evidence and discredit those who wish to use the evidence to speak out.

The first example involves a ship log from the U.S.S. *Curtiss* detailing a UFO sighting during nuclear testing in the South Pacific. From March through May 1954, a series of atomic weapon tests took place at the Pacific Proving Grounds under the designation Operation Castle. The testing was at Bikini Atoll in the Marshall Islands. The U.S.S. *Curtiss* was a support ship for the operation. On April 7, 1954, the ship log listed a sighting of an unidentified flying object passing over the ship. Researcher Robert Hastings, while writing *UFOs and Nukes: Extraordinary Encounters at Nuclear Weapons Sites,* was alerted to the ship log reference in 2004.[171]

When Hastings went on the U.S. Department of Energy (DOE) website, he found that the ship log transcript still contained the UFO reference. Having downloaded a copy of the ship's log, the entry reads as follows:

> "7 April ... at 0408 on station in operating area BH 35-40-L; Steamed independently in operating area BG 28-36-L; At 1138 anchored berth N-6, Bikini; at 1948 left berth en route to Eniwetok; **at 2305 hours an unidentified luminous object passed over the ship from bow to stern, yellowish-orange in color, traveling at a high rate of speed and a low altitude.**"[172] (*emphasis added.*)

Later, in December 2004, Hastings again tried to access the ship log entry and found it missing. Not just the one page, but many pages before and after the UFO entry were now missing. In 1998, 2000, and early 2004, the pages, which mostly contained innocuous ship movement information, were still on the official DOE website. The missing pages included page 341 that had the UFO reference. Obviously, someone had deleted them. Now, the URL contains a single, unrelated 1953 letter.

The original ship log pages were reviewed by several veterans who were researching an unrelated topic, veteran's health issues. From discovery by a veteran's health advocate in 1998, the pages

---

[171] Hastings, Robert, *UFOs and Nukes: Extraordinary Encounters at Nuclear Weapons Sites,* AuthorHouse (2008), pp. 97–104. Mr. Hastings learned of the ship log reference from Patrick Broudy, Legislative Director of National Association of Atomic Veterans, who found it while conducting research in 1998.

[172] Ibid. @ p. 99, Defense Nuclear Agency (DNA), Castle Series, 1954, DNA 6035F, United States Atmospheric Weapons Tests, p. 341.

containing the ship log entry remained intact until December 2004. They did not disappear until after a UFO researcher accessed them.

Assuming that the "unidentified luminous object" was intelligently controlled, its sighting during a nuclear weapons test would confirm that its occupants were interested in our nuclear weapons. It is hard to believe that the ship log reference was not a matter of defense interest. The object was in a position to observe one of our secret weapons tests.

Another example comes from an incident involving a cargo plane that encountered unusual objects over Alaska. On November 17, 1986, evidence of a UFO encounter with a Japan Airlines (JAL) jet was recorded on radar by the Federal Aviation Administration (FAA). A Boing 747 cargo plane got permission from Anchorage flight control to take evasive action to avoid a walnut-shaped object the size of an aircraft carrier, with smaller objects the size of commercial passenger jets emerging from it.[173]

The FAA launched an air safety investigation of the matter. In Alaska, an FAA official interviewed the JAL flight crew about the incident shortly after they landed. A follow-up interview was conducted by two FAA special agents.[174] Both military and civilian radar tracked the incident for 31 minutes. Eventually, the FAA issued confusing and contradictory explanations. According to a senior FAA official, the CIA took the evidence.

John Callahan, the FAA Division Chief of the Accidents and Investigations branch, has stated that, the day after the incident, the FBI and CIA sent officials to be briefed at the FAA Washington,

---

[173] Clark, Jerome, *The UFO Book: Encyclopedia of the Extraterrestrial*, Visible Ink Press (1998), pp. 315–318.

[174] Ibid, @ p 317.

D.C. headquarters.[175] At the briefing, the CIA ordered the FAA "to turn over its radar, air traffic voice communications, and written records related to the incident."[176] Callahan, who reviewed the radar tapes and kept a copy, has been a vocal critic of how the CIA interfered with an investigation of a significant air safety incident.[177] What he saw was a UFO chasing a 747 for 30 minutes.

The CIA classified the radar materials at a meeting of the FAA, FBI, and members of the White House Science Advisor Office. The CIA representatives were from the Office of Scientific Intelligence. OSI was the same CIA branch that had responsibility over the 1953 Robertson Panel. Callahan was in the back of the room and was inadvertently not sworn to secrecy.

This incident shows that the CIA OSI was still interested in UFOs in 1986. OSI was still involved 33 years after the Robertson Panel set the policy to "debunk" UFOs. This contradicts the CIA's official history of its involvement with UFOs written in 1990.[178] Either an FAA Division Chief of Accidents and Investigations was lying, or the CIA still had the legal ability to classify UFO evidence over U.S. airspace based on national security concerns. What would be the motive of a career accident investigator, with no prior interest in the UFO phenomenon, to tell such a story if it were not true?

---

[175] Hastings, Robert, *UFOs and Nukes: Extraordinary Encounters at Nuclear Weapons Sites*, AuthorHouse (2008), pp. 185–186.

[176] Ibid, @ p. 185. Mr. Callahan has been interviewed about the incident and subsequent cover up. https://www.youtube.com/watch?v=HUak1jfA2Hg.

[177] https://nationalufocenter.com/2013/12/ufos-are-real-faa-division-chief-john-callahan-2010/

[178] Haines, Gerald K., *CIA's Role in the Study of UFOs, 1947–90: A Die-Hard Issue,* https://www.cia.gov/readingroom/document/0005517742.

If the former FAA Chief of Air Safety Investigations claim is accurate, this incident means that the CIA Office of Scientific Intelligence still had the authority to overrule an FAA safety review and the President's own science advisor. This role reversal puts the CIA in charge of a domestic incident (Alaska) involving air safety. It also puts the CIA in a supervisory role over what evidence could be used by the White House Science Advisor to educate the President on a matter of air safety.

Under Article II of the Constitution, the President has authority over the executive branch of government. This includes the FAA and CIA. Each supposedly report to the President. Here, it seems that the tail was wagging the dog with a security oath given to a White House official. This was evidence of a lengthy incident that caused a commercial airliner to take evasive action. If John Callahan had signed the security oath, we would never have known about this incident. It appears that air safety takes a back seat to keeping evidence of UFOs out of the public eye.

Another incident of disappearing evidence occurred in October 2011. An Air Force manual (Air Force Instruction 10-206) contained a chapter on recovery of downed UFOs. Chapter Five applied to UFOs that were subject to special procedures not applicable to terrestrial aircraft. Government document researcher John Greenewald, Jr. wrote about how Chapter Five disappeared from the DoD website in his recent book about government secrecy.[179] While the DoD manual was available to the public from at least 2001, it took significant knowledge of its website to find it. John was the person one would expect to find such hidden information.

Mr. Greenewald, one of the unsung heroes of public disclosure, has run a website documenting government records on a wide

---

[179] Greenewald, John, *Inside the Black Vault: The Government's UFO Secrets Revealed*, Rowan & Littlefield (2019), Chapter 14 (The Greatest Trick of a Magician).

variety of topics called the *Black Vault*.[180] His passion for researching government records, originally UFO records, started in high school. At age 16, he received a visit from two FBI agents inquiring about his interest in government records, much to the surprise of his parents.

In October 2011, he received a call from *Huffington Post* journalist Lee Spiegel. Spiegel asked Greenewald about what he thought were the most interesting UFO documents he had discovered.[181] After discussing the Air Force manual (Air Force Instruction 10-206, Chapter 5), Greenewald walked the reporter through the website. After Mr. Spiegel found Chapter Five, he called the Pentagon, asking for comment. No one was available to take his call, and he left messages requesting comment. By the next day, Chapter Five was missing, and the Air Force spokesperson claimed it had been removed as part of a routine update process. It was eventually replaced by a chapter on hurricane recovery procedures. The Air Force's explanation for the removal of Chapter Five contained numerous spelling errors, indicating the haste with which the Air Force posted the notice. It is highly unlikely a planned 2011 website update occurred between the *Huffington Post* inquiry and the next day. It had been on the Air Force website for at least 10 years.

John Greenewald experienced the same "scrubbing" of the DoD website as Robert Hastings had with the Department of Energy website. Once the DoD is alerted to interest in UFO-related documents, they are immediately removed from public view. With Greenewald, it was a set of protocols that documented how the military would clean up after a UFO crash. Since Mr. Greenewald downloaded Chapter Five before it was erased, one can see it on his website, *The Black Vault*. It mentions procedures meant to protect

---

[180] https://www.theblackvault.com.

[181] Greenewald, John, *Inside the Black Vault: The Government's UFO Secrets Revealed*, Rowan & Littlefield (2019), pp. 151–154.

personnel from contamination by crash debris. Just having a chapter on downed UFO crash recovery procedures means that there are national security concerns. Once the *Huffington Post* left messages with the Air Force requesting comment, the item was quickly deleted.

The fact that a UFO-specific chapter was available to the public was probably unintentional. Once Air Force personnel learned of its public availability, they quickly removed it. It was a separate chapter from those that dealt with terrestrial-based crashes where debris was recovered. Since a reporter asked for comment, the Air Force personnel could not just delete it without an explanation. An explanation used the familiar response of "routine maintenance." However, one would assume that a "routine" act of website maintenance would use better grammar in its one paragraph announcement.

As was the case for Robert Hastings, the government could not demand the return of all copies of the mysterious Chapter Five. This would have set off more alarm bells. The removal had to have a public explanation, however implausible.

The Hastings book and the *Black Vault* both show the contradiction between the professed policy of "no security threat" and the government's actual conduct. Overall, the three incidents (1986, 2004 & 2011) show that the government still acts quickly to remove evidence from the public domain, if there is any hint that the public has access. From the perspective of Callahan (1986), Hastings (2004), and Greenewald (2011), they are deprived of the ability to defend their narrative because of government interference. They also had their speech rights interfered with by the removal of evidence meant to undercut their arguments on a public policy issue.

Each instance is an example of a "prior restraint" of speech. Callahan, Hastings, and Greenewald could still talk about documentary evidence that was in the public domain. In Callahan's case, he could still talk about the radar tapes after his retirement. Greenewald can talk about the saga of the missing Chapter Five and Hastings about the missing ship logs. However, their stories are undercut by simple counterclaims that the copies they possess are mere hoaxes like photographs discussed herein. These incidents show how the government, even after a mistake is made, can undercut the credibility of a witness. Each instance shows the longevity of the Robertson Panel's "debunking" policy. In order to maintain these policies over a long period of time, there needs to be a logistical infrastructure in place to handle these "problems" as they arise. The next chapter discusses more evidence about the length of these programs.

CHAPTER SEVENTEEN

DISAPPEARING AND REAPPEARING POLAROIDS

On August 3, 1965, an Orange County, California road department highway safety engineer was making his rounds. Rex Heflin was looking into a safety concern when he noticed a strange object hovering close to his pickup truck. He had a Polaroid camera with him and took three pictures of the craft. He got out of his truck and took a fourth picture of a strange smoke ring that remained after the object departed.[182]

Heflin, who had no previous interest in UFOs, showed them to co-workers. They were impressed with his three photos of the UFO. However, they scoffed at the fourth photo of the "smoke ring." After this reaction from his co-workers about the fourth photo, he did not show it around for years. He had assumed that the object was an experimental craft from nearby El Toro Marine Base.

Thereafter, he loaned the three photos to relatives. Eventually, thanks to a relative, the *Santa Ana Register* (now *Orange County Register*) published his photos and forever associated Mr. Heflin's name with UFOs. Each was a clear representation of a UFO that was shaped like the straw boater hats that were popular in the early 20th century. Since the photos were taken by a self-developing Polaroid camera, it would have taken significant effort to fake the photos. As Heflin did not assume the object was a UFO or seek

---

[182] There are many accounts of Mr. Heflin's encounter. Likely, the most detailed was written by Ann Druffel, a member of NICAP, for *UFO Magazine* in August 2006, pp. 52–63. (www.nicap.org/reports/Goodbye_Rex_Heflin.pdf.); *see also*, https://www.youtube.com/watch?v=rzVgrCCVpH0.

publicity, it is difficult to see why he would fake the pictures while on duty for his government employer.

Once word about the three UFO photos spread, Heflin loaned the originals to a succession of service branches. The Marine Corp, Navy, and Air Force borrowed and returned the photos showing the UFO. The fourth photo, showing only a smoke ring, was never loaned out. However, everything changed for Heflin once the photos were published in the local newspaper. Immediately after the September 20, 1965 publication of the photos, Heflin was approached for a fourth time by men claiming to represent the North American Aerospace Defense Command (NORAD), a combined Canadian/American defense organization. As before, he loaned his three original Polaroid UFO photos to the men who had shown him fake military identifications. After not hearing back from them, he called NORAD. NORAD denied any involvement in the incident, leaving Mr. Heflin with a mystery, but no photos.

Heflin's case followed a familiar pattern for those who captured compelling photographic UFO evidence. First, he had no prior interest in the subject. Second, he was asked to turn over the original photos of the craft to military officials. Third, the photos were not returned. Fourth, there was a denial by authorities that they were involved in any tampering or theft. This saga follows the path discussed in Chapter Fifteen of photos given over to "trusted" government officials.

The two "NORAD" men had gone to great lengths to obtain the photographs. They had to find where Heflin lived. Employing fake IDs, and, despite wearing civilian clothes, they pretended to represent NORAD. The timing shows that two days before the photos were misappropriated, the *Santa Ana Register* story with his three photos had run. Publicity seems to be the key element that led to the theft, as has been in other cases.

The act of impersonating a military officer to obtain the photographs is a federal crime. Any person "who pretends to be an officer" of the United States and "obtains any ... document or thing of value" has committed a felony.[183] These acts were crimes, regardless of whether they were actual federal employees. One government employee cannot masquerade as a different official to obtain private property. Mr. Heflin had not committed a crime and was not under suspicion of wrongdoing. He merely took some photos that were later disseminated by others.

If the fake NORAD officers were government agents, their actions violated Rex Heflin's constitutional rights. First, they took his property without due process or payment of the reasonable compensation for the photos. Second, they did so under false pretenses in violation of a federal statute. Third, they cautioned him to not speak about the matter, which is an attempt to restrain his free speech rights. Acting under the color of federal authority, the two men conspired to deprive Heflin of his property rights and the best evidence to defend himself against charges that he hoaxed the photos. Fortunately for Heflin, his work reputation did not suffer, and he remained a valued employee of the Orange County road department until his disability-related retirement. Throughout this period, Mr. Heflin did not try to profit off the photos. He freely loaned them out to family members and showed them to his co-workers. He never sought renumeration and did not have them copyrighted.

Unfortunately, the Project Blue Book investigation of the three photos fit the pattern of similar cases. Before the NORAD men, the first contact for Blue Book was by Captain Charles F. Reichmuth from AFOSI, the same Air Force department that took Joseph Perry's photo five years earlier. He took the three photos, made copies, and returned the originals to Heflin. He interviewed Heflin's co-workers and supervisors, learning he was a trustworthy employee. Reichmuth's report to Project Blue Book was that

---

[183] 18 United States Code § 912.

Heflin's three photos were of an object of unknown origin and not a hoax.[184]

The personnel at Project Blue Book, without further investigation, came to a different conclusion. This conclusion was based on copies of the photos, since the originals had been returned to Heflin by Captain Reichmuth. Blue Book, from its offices at Wright-Patterson Air Force Base in Columbus, Ohio, declared that the photos were fraudulent. Blue Book, apparently unable to debunk the photos, claimed they were faked. No one from Blue Book interviewed Mr. Heflin, nor did any further investigation besides reviewing the report and copies of the three photographs made by Captain Reichmuth.

Heflin was not given any means to contest the Air Force Blue Book determination. Without the original photos, he was hardly in a position to defend his reputation. As with others who had filmed a UFO, he was defined by the pictures he took. Official government records state that he perpetrated a hoax. A hoax to support a phenomenon he had no interest in before being involuntarily swept into the public eye. He was accused of hoaxing pictures of what he had initially thought was an experimental aircraft.

Decades after their disappearance at the hands of the "NORAD" men, the photos were eventually returned to Rex Heflin in a mysterious manner. Heflin had retired and moved to Northern California. Because of his exposure to pollutants from years of working on roadways, he was plagued by poor health until he eventually succumbed to cancer in 2005. Before he passed away, he got his photographs returned. The late pioneering UFO researcher Ann Druffel explained the return as follows:

> "One day in 1993, the phone rang in his Northern
> California home. A woman's voice asked, 'Have you

---

[184] www.nicap.org/reports/Goodbye_Rex_Heflin.pdf; *UFO Magazine* @ pp. 54–55.

checked your mailbox lately?' Then the call was abruptly terminated. He went to the mailbox and found it empty. About a half-hour later, the same unidentified woman called again with the same question, hanging up immediately.

Heflin went out to his mailbox again and found a plain 9 by 12-inch manila envelope with no postage or other marks indicating manner of delivery. Inside, he found the long-lost originals of photos 1, 2, and 3 that had been taken by the "NORAD men" in 1965!"[185]

The three returned photos matched markings on the fourth photo that Heflin had retained. The photos, from 1965 until 1993, were in the possession of someone else. At least three people were involved, not including the mystery delivery person, during their 28-year hiatus. Whether they were held by the federal government is an open question.

When the photos were returned to Heflin, the damage was already done. Nearly 28 years of conflicting opinions by "experts" who were working off of copies of the original photographs left the legacy of the sighting in limbo. What were arguably among the best UFO photos have now become a minor footnote in history. Recent analysis of the four original photos shows that each photo had the same cloud-covered background, with no discernable abnormalities that would indicate a hoax.[186] Accurate depiction of a UFO or not, the original photos were kept out of public circulation by unknown persons carrying fake government identification cards. Whoever these agents worked for; the

---

[185] www.nicap.org/reports/Goodbye_Rex_Heflin.pdf; *UFO Magazine* @ p. 61 (August 2006).

[186] Armentano, Dom, "OC's moment in UFO History," *Orange County Register* (October 30, 2009) (https://www.ocregister.com/2009/10/30/ocs-moment-in-ufo-history/).

organization was still in existence in 1993. This organization tracked Rex Heflin into his retirement and was able to return the pictures to a sick man when the likelihood of their widespread use had long since passed.

CHAPTER EIGHTEEN

AMERICAN PSYCHOLOGICAL WARFARE

The first morning of the Robertson Panel did not begin with a discussion of the unknown aerial phenomenon. After introductions, Marine/CIA Intelligence Officer Philip Strong explained that the danger did not come from the phenomenon, but from people who paid attention to it.

The "indirect" dangers were the claimed psychological reactions that average citizens have to flying saucers. However, there were no witnesses with any expertise in psychology, sociology, or psychiatry. The Panel's recommendation was that citizen panic was the real risk from flying saucers. This finding was preordained, having been developed months before by the Air Force and the CIA, with still-classified input from the CIA Psychological Review Board.

The "indirect dangers" were addressed with a plan to change the behavior of the public. By reducing the number of quality witnesses and evidence, the Air Force would become the only authoritative source on UFOs. When rare cases broke into the traditional media, the government narrative would be without quality opposition. The Air Force and CIA wanted to clear the field of pilots, academics, and other trained observers who would be trusted by the public. This allowed the Air Force to speak virtually unchallenged, with each case having a simple explanation, as long as nobody looked too closely. Until December 2017, these deliberate efforts to influence the public and Congress worked well enough to keep UAP from becoming a serious public policy issue.

The Robertson Panel was made up of a distinguished cast of scientists who worked on weapons development during and after

World War II. None, however, had any background in psychology that would help them assess "mass hysteria and panic" arguments. They addressed the "mass hysteria and panic" arguments with two recommendations: debunking and public education. The public education component, developed independently by the Panel, was never implemented. However, the clandestine debunking idea recommended by the CIA was adopted. The Robertson Panel's comments on public education were as follows:

> "The 'debunking' aim would result in a reduction in public interest in 'flying saucers' which today evokes a strong psychological reaction. This education could be accomplished by mass media, such as television, motion pictures, and popular articles. The basis of such education would be actual case histories which had been puzzling at first but later explained. As in the case of conjuring tricks, there is much less stimulation if the 'secret' is known. Such a program should tend to reduce the current gullibility of the public and consequently their susceptibility to clever hostile propaganda."[187]

One of the goals of the Panel's public education recommendation was to use the media to educate the public, which would "reduce the gullibility of the public." A mass media public education program would use psychologists to implement this recommendation. However, no psychologists were ever used. In fact, the Federal Civil Defense Administration (FCDA) was informed of the Robertson Panel recommendations but never started a program. If the CIA and Air Force wanted a public education program to address the use of flying saucers to mask a

---

[187] https://www.cia.gov/readingroom/docs/DOC_0000015458.pdf @ pp. 15–16. This quote is from the version released on October 5, 1978. Later versions of the "Comments and Suggestions" have language not included in this version. For instance, the 1994 version, released to the Center on UFO Studies, has the quote on pages 19–20 with many additions not found in the 1978 version. (http://www.cufon.org/cufon/robert.htm.)

Soviet attack, the FCDA would have been the logical choice to implement it. Except for being told about the recommendations after the Panel was finished, Civil Defense was never involved. Instead, declassified records show the Air Force and CIA chose to clandestinely interfere with free speech and other constitutional rights to help condition the public to ignore UFOs.

From the first CIA/Air Force meeting in August 1952, the subject of Soviet intentions was claimed to be at the core of the need for psychological warfare tools. Yet, the Panel found no evidence that the Soviet Union had used flying saucers as a propaganda tool or even allowed coverage of the subject in its state-controlled press. The Panel gave this absence of evidence a sinister connotation. Regardless of the lack of evidence, the Soviet Union must have been cooking something up to use flying saucers to mask an invasion. Using this unlikely narrative, the CIA got what it wanted. The resulting recommendation gave the CIA and Air Force the green light to influence information seen by ordinary Americans. It was the same media that many of its members were receiving payments from the CIA for favorable press coverage.[188]

With the "public education" component ignored, the CIA and Air Force plunged ahead to implement the "debunking" recommendations. Within three weeks, the CIA, with the help of the FBI, became the catalyst behind the collapse of Civilian Saucer Investigators (Los Angeles). This group was likely the best source of non-governmental scientific information at the time. By 1954, they were out of business. Simultaneously, the Air Force put pressure on commercial airlines and pilots to stop reporting flying saucer sightings to the press. This was done through persuasion aimed at commercial airlines and formal regulations that stifled free

---

[188] Bernstein, Carl, "The CIA and the Media," *Rolling Stone Magazine*, October 20, 1977, pp. 55–67.

speech of the pilots. As a result, the number of pilots that talked about sightings dwindled to zero by the late 1950s.

People who voluntarily came forward with quality photographs were treated harshly. This book has chronicled typical cases intended to denigrate people possessing critical evidence. If the evidence and credibility of the witness were too strong, the Air Force would simply brand them a "hoaxer," like Rex Heflin. Those who were so branded had no recourse to protect their reputations. The Air Force policy was to slander people. Even the FBI, which helped start the debunking program, did not want to be associated with these tactics.

Given the times, this reading of the intentions of the Air Force, FBI, and CIA would hardly be novel. In the 1970s, the United States Senate Select Committee on Intelligence Activities Within the United States (Church Committee) found many instances of similar illegal conduct, much of it beginning in 1953. The Church Committee's final report summarized its results as follows:

> "We have examined three types of 'intelligence' activities affecting the rights of American citizens. The first is intelligence collection – such as infiltrating groups with informants, wiretapping, or opening letters. The second is dissemination of material that is collected. **The third is covert action designed to disrupt and discredit the activities of groups and individuals deemed a threat to the social order.**"[189] (*emphasis added.*)

When looking at the conclusions of the Robertson Panel, many of them match the findings of the Church Committee. It justified the same or similar crimes committed by the same agencies, and

---

[189] U.S. Senate Select Committee on Intelligence Activities Within the United States, *Intelligence Activities and the Rights of Americans: 1976 U.S. Senate Report on Illegal Wiretaps and Domestic Spying by the FBI, CIA and NSA*, Red and Black Publishers (2007), p. 7.

during the same time period. For example, the Robertson Panel conclusion 3(a) reads:

> "That the continued emphasis on the reporting of these phenomenon does, in these parlous times, result in a threat to the orderly functioning of the protective organs of the body politic."

The Church Committee highlighted three areas of illegal activity conducted by the CIA and the FBI. One was the domestic covert efforts to disrupt lawful groups because they were "deemed a threat to the social order." These efforts were mostly made at lower levels of government without paperwork or the knowledge of elected officials. Among the illegal CIA programs conducted during this period were the MK-Ultra mind control program, payments to journalists, and domestic letter-opening operations. Each lasted for decades. The CIA programs began under the leadership of Allen Dulles. Implementation of these "debunking" efforts also began with the help of the FBI. Director J. Edgar Hoover was one of the first people outside of the Air Force and CIA to learn of the program. Hoover learned of the Panel recommendations, having attended a January 30, 1953 briefing to the CIA ONE program. After the briefing, he immediately sent an FBI agent to meet with Dr. Riedel and "persuade" him to give up his UFO study.

The Church Committee revealed other efforts of the CIA and FBI that undermined free speech. In a summary of its findings and conclusions, the Church Report stated as follows:

> "The First Amendment protects the Rights of American citizens to engage in free and open discussions, and to associate with persons of their own choosing. Intelligence agencies have, on

occasion, expressly attempted to interfere with those rights."[190]

Early in the process, CIA staff discussed how they would minimize paperwork to improve efficiency in their UFO efforts. The Church Committee, reviewing numerous illegal programs over its 40-year review period, noted that a common element to many of these programs was the inability to establish upper level accountability.[191] These illegal programs had little or no paperwork documenting their actions.

The CIA deliberately chose not to advocate a public element for its debunking aim. In fact, the CIA's main intent was to hide its involvement. After knowledge leaked that a panel of scientists had studied UFOs, NICAP made a concerted effort to get an unredacted copy of the scientific panel's work product. A meeting was held on March 16, 1958 to discuss how to respond to this request.[192]

The discussion centered on the potential release of the Robertson Panel Report to NICAP's Dr. Leon Davidson. In order to keep the CIA's name out of the press, a declassified version was released through the Air Force without reference to the CIA. Several of the Panel members had voiced objections if their names were tied to the CIA. On behalf of the CIA, Philip Strong suggested an approach intended to limit future questions about UFOs.[193] The claimed reason for secrecy had to do with the Panel's recommendations about the "dangerous consequences to national

---

[190] Ibid, @ p. 20.

[191] Ibid, @ p. 17–18. The Air Force and CIA staffs agreed that their goal would be to minimize the amount of paperwork in this endeavor. "Flying Saucers Problem," October 14, 1952, CIA-RDP81R00560R000100020010-9.pdf.

[192] "Meeting with Air Force Personnel Concerning Advisory Scientific Panel Concerning Unidentified Flying Objects," dated May 16, 1958. DOC 005516044. (Declassified in 2010.)

[193] Ibid, @ p. 1, para. 5.

security." Yet, at the time, the Air Force had completed its radar net in the Arctic, which eliminated any need to rely on civilian assistance for observation. In fact, the Civilian Observer Corps had disbanded. The secrecy was more about protecting CIA involvement and the faulty premise that the "debunking" recommendations were based upon. Legislative counsel was more interested in keeping the matter quiet and away from congressional scrutiny.

Instead, we are left with policies designed to ridicule UFO witnesses. The tactics employed by the Air Force, FBI, and CIA post-Robertson Panel focused on ridicule of a small group of people with one thing in common rather than educating the general public. The first approach to Dr. Riedel of North American Aviation, according to the FBI contact memo, highlighted how professional organizations would frown on his UFO activities. The attempt showed that the appeal for him to stop investigating UFOs was because of professional embarrassment to the scientist. Yet, this message was conveyed by a federal agent to a scientist that owed his job in California to a clandestine program. Later, in 1953, a CIA status memo talks about multiple actions taken by the Agency that were partially successful. By 1958, the CIA was still worried about the public finding out about its involvement. As late as 1986, the CIA engaged in keeping UFO evidence from being made public according to the FAA's chief accident investigator. However, the 1990 CIA official history of its UFO involvement states it was no longer involved in UFO matters long before the 1986 FAA/JAL/Alaska incident.

Meanwhile, the Air Force, as the public face of government UFO efforts, was also taking steps to marginalize the phenomenon. It adopted regulations that made it a crime for pilots to talk about UFO sightings. Instead, the pilots had to report sightings in a form that would subject them to scrutiny by the Air Force and threaten their flight status. Simultaneously, the Air Force, according to news service reports, had told commercial air carriers to stop their pilots from speaking to the press about UFO sightings. If a pilot did speak out about a quality sighting, they would have to file an Air Force report. The Air Force follow up would fall into one of three categories. Either the pilot was mistaken, delusional, or was perpetrating a hoax. None of these options would be good for their careers.

Persons who took quality photographs usually fell into the hoax category. Those who took these pictures had much in common. Before they took their pictures, they had no interest in UFOs. Each was happy to talk to federal authorities, intending to help the government out. In return, they had their pictures destroyed, called out as attempting to defraud the government, and faced ridicule for life by being branded in this way. In one incident, this conduct continued for at least 27 years until Rex Heflin was given his photos back through mysterious circumstances.

The common denominator behind this "debunking" strategy was ridicule of American citizens who had no way of fighting back. The use of ridicule to gain obedience for the prevailing social order is as old as civilization itself. Ridicule is a two-edged sword. On one hand, the citizenry can use it to mock its own government. On the other hand, it can be used as a tool of government to ridicule those who do not stay within societal norms.[194] Using a phrase that became popular in the 1950s, it was "psychological warfare" intended to shape public opinion. As stated by the Robertson Panel, the goal of the CIA was "to strip the Unidentified Flying Objects of the special status they have been given and the aura of mystery they have unfortunately acquired."

---

[194] *i.e.,* Billig, Michael, *Laughter and Ridicule: Towards a Social Critique of Humor,* Sage Publications (2005). Social scientist Professor Billig chronicles the use of humor in a variety of settings. Chapter Nine ("Embarrassment, Humor and the Social Order") discusses how ridicule has been used to keep people within the bounds of the approved social order.

The way to tear down the "special status" that UFOs had acquired was to tear down the people who report or study them. The recommendation of a scientific panel was used to give credibility to goals under the guise of the fight against communism. While the Robertson Panel was made up of distinguished physical scientists, the "debunking" recommendation required social science expertise. One would not hire a physicist or astronomer to give you an expert opinion about the possibility of "mass hysteria," "hysterical behavior," or a "morbid national psychology." The still-classified input of the CIA Psychological Strategy Review Board likely had a hand in the direction toward "debunking."

As stated in the Church Committee Report, the 1950s were a time when abuses were conducted in the name of national security. Unlike today, there was no congressional committee dedicated to oversight of the intelligence community. Even within the Eisenhower Administration, the CIA updates varied based on who was getting the information. These external reports did not focus on the methods or goals related to "debunking." Only internal CIA documents detailed its attempt to shape the topics that Americans can talk about without being ridiculed.

The question today is whether these efforts are continuing? Since the declassified documents from the 50s and 60s are just now being released, it is difficult to determine whether there still is an effort to denigrate people with an interest in the phenomenon. However, one need to look no further than the CIA website to get indications that the policy of debunking has not changed in the intervening years.

In 2007, the CIA posted on its website the previously written official history of its involvement in the UFO phenomenon.[195] The document admits some early involvement, but states that the

---

[195] Haines, Gerald K., *CIA's Role in the Study of UFOs, 1947–90: A Die-Hard Issue*, (posted: April 14, 2007).

Agency has had minimal to no involvement since the 1950s. Besides its many inaccuracies about the phenomenon, the official history continues the "debunking" policy by denigrating those who have an interest in the UFO phenomenon. It begins by describing those who study UFOs as "UFO buffs." The term "buff" describes "enthusiasts" who engage in a hobby, like model train "buffs." In other words, the term denotes a fascination with a subject that has no serious implications but only intended to amuse. As used in this manner, the term "buff" was intended to denigrate an entire field of endeavor as not worthy to be of legitimate public policy concern. Yet, NICAP, the largest UFO organization at the time, was advocating for Congress to hold hearings. The First Amendment does not allow the federal government to pick winners and losers about what people believe should be subject to policy debate. The only purpose behind this labeling on the CIA website was to denigrate speakers who disagree with the government UFO policy.

The CIA history also gives a brief explanation of the events leading up to the formation of the Robertson Panel, including referencing its "mass hysteria" finding. This history diverges from the declassified record regarding actions taken after the conclusion of the Robertson Panel. It specifically mentions that Todos M. Odarenko "did not want to take on the problem" because of his heavy workload. According to the CIA history, he was against storing files that monitored UFOs. However, this claim is contradicted by the year-end report written by Odarenko that detailed the positive and negative results of following the Robertson Panel recommendations.[196] This memo, released in February 2010, directly contradicts the CIA UFO history claim that it only monitored the phenomenon thereafter. The heavily redacted 1953 memo talked about "actions" taken to implement the Robertson Panel Report. The contact memo about scientist Dr.

---

[196] "Current Status of Unidentified Flying Objects," (UFOB), December 17, 1953, DOC 0005515979.

Walther Riedel also contradicts the "monitor-only" claims found in the official CIA history.

Later in the history's 1950s portion, there is much written about the efforts by NICAP member, Dr. Leon Davidson, to obtain CIA records. The history mentions that Dr. Davidson was seeking information that would show CIA involvement with the Robertson Panel. The "official history" refers to him in disparaging terms and downplays official documented efforts to hide the truth of CIA involvement.[197]

While discussing the "pressure" that one person, Leon Davidson, was putting on the CIA and Air Force to come clean about CIA involvement, the official history fails to cite the May 18, 1958 meeting where a CIA lawyer met with involved personnel to determine how to respond to Davidson without setting off alarm bells in Congress.[198] The meeting memorandum was not declassified until 2010 and shows that the official history either cherry-picked information that casts the CIA efforts in the best possible light or it failed to take into account classified information. From all appearances, the reason for the original classification of this May 16, 1958 memorandum appears to relate to covering up CIA involvement rather than national security needs.

Throughout the official UFO/CIA history, Davidson's request is treated with disrespect. Dr. Davidson "had convinced himself" that the Agency was involved with the phenomenon. In fact, the CIA was involved as declassified records now show. Without evidence, it was suggested that Davidson's interests were sinister

---

[197] Haines, Gerald K., "CIA's Role in the Study of UFOs, 1947–90: A Die-Hard Issue." (posted: April 14, 2007), see: subheading, CIA's U-2 and OXCART as UFOs, pp.73–75, https://www.cia.gov/static/cia-role-study-UFOs.pdf.

[198] Meeting with Air Force Personnel Concerning Advisory Scientific Panel Concerning Unidentified Flying Objects, dated 17 January 1953, May 16, 1958. DOC 005516044. (Declassified in 2010.)

with "some of them perhaps not in the best interest of this country...." This aspersion is consistent with the "threat" scenario aimed at persons who contest the CIA/Air Force narrative about UFOs.

Overall, the narrative about the involvement of Dr. Davidson portrays him as a pest. One cannot find another example where a citizen making legitimate inquiries for government information is lampooned this way on a government website. The narrative goes on to state that "(i)n another attempt to pacify Davidson," a CIA officer dressed up as an Air Force officer to meet with him. Davidson was "incensed over what he perceived was a runaround." In fact, he was getting the runaround by the CIA through illegal tactics, including posing as a military officer (violation of federal law). With the contact, the CIA officer was also engaging in "internal-security functions" prohibited by law.

The denigration of Dr. Leon Davidson is still prominently posted on the CIA's historical archive website, indicating their "debunking" priority continues.[199] With Davidson, the CIA aimed their fire at a very accomplished American. Dr. Davidson worked on the Manhattan Project during World War II. He later was a consultant to the Oak Ridge National Laboratories. Davidson was also involved in early work with computers for several large corporations, including IBM as their manager of advanced applications. His interest in UFOs was personal, believing they were U.S. secret weapons. He was able to convince a congressional committee to gain the public release of Project Blue Book's computer-generated Special Report Number 14. Instead of being a pest, he had the kind of resume similar to members of the Robertson Panel. It is a sad commentary that the CIA continues to denigrate

---

[199] https://www.cia.gov/resources/csi/studies-in-intelligence/studies-in-intelligence-1997/cias-role-in-the-study-of-ufos-1947-1990/.

such a successful American, all because he studied UFOs in his spare time.

Ironically, Dr. Davidson volunteered in the 1950s at the Civil Defense Filter Center that helped identify aircraft over the crowded airspace of the New York metropolitan area. Quite a twist of fate that he was volunteering to identify aircraft while working with groups that the Robertson Panel said would create "panic" and "mass hysteria" by misidentifying flying objects.

Later in the "official history," it continues to claim a lack of CIA involvement after the early years of the phenomenon. However, its involvement extended decades into the future, as demonstrated by the FAA's Division Chief of Accidents and Investigations, John Callahan. He was present at a 1986 meeting where CIA officials classified flight information about a UFO incident where evidence relevant to an FAA air safety investigation was seized. Either the CIA narrative is incorrect, or a high-ranking career aviation official lied about the incident. Since the CIA official history is inaccurate in a number of respects, a strong inference can be drawn that the CIA was still involved in the UFO phenomenon well beyond the time period listed on the CIA website.

The real reason for the CIA reticence to explain its involvement cannot be founded on embarrassment alone. Evidence in declassified records and the testimony of highly credible witnesses shows that the CIA used illegal tactics to control the free speech rights of Americans to protect the "no national security threat" policy. The question today is whether this policy continues. Evidence indicates that the answer is "Yes." It is still continuing.

The recent *Preliminary Assessment: Unidentified Aerial Phenomena*, issued on June 25, 2021, uses official ridicule as an excuse for the lack of reports of UAPs. This excuse was stated as follows:

"UAP Collection Challenges

Sociocultural stigmas and sensor limitations remain obstacles to collecting data on UAP.... Narratives from aviators in the operational community and analysts from the military and IC describe disparagement associated with observing UAP, reporting it, or attempting to discuss it with colleagues. Although the effects of these stigmas have lessened as senior members of the scientific, policy, military, and intelligence communities engage on the topic seriously in public, reputational risk may keep many observers silent, complicating scientific pursuit of the topic." [200]

The Office of the Director of National Intelligence (ODNI) used ridicule as an excuse for a lack of UAP reports. Ridicule that was the product of government policy. The Robertson Panel and Air Force policies are still contributing to a lack of witness reports. Consider that the military pilot reports come almost exclusively from Navy pilots, not Air Force pilots. The past policy impact is still slowing government efforts, especially in the service branch that was most involved with the phenomenon. The irony is hard to miss.

While there are many incidents found in the declassified record, surely there is more evidence that has yet to be released. However, information from private UFO researchers may also provide leads showing other "debunking" conduct. One such incident concerns a set of documents that may show a long-term, organized "debunking" effort. Since the 1980s, information has mysteriously surfaced, linking government efforts of either a hidden government UAP program or revealing a long-term disinformation campaign. This information might reveal an actual government program controlling secret UFO activities. More likely, the whole thing was an elaborate disinformation campaign.

---

[200] ODNI, *Preliminary Assessment: Unidentified Aerial Phenomena* @ p. 4 (June 25, 2021).

The drama started when UFO researchers began receiving mysterious documents showing a secretive government program, known as Majestic Twelve (MJ-12). The documents allege that MJ-12 controlled all aspects of the U.S. response to the phenomenon. Detractors claim that the documents are fake. Their authenticity has divided the UFO research community for decades. Now, the legislatively mandated historical review may shed light on the origins of the MJ-12 documents. Are they real? If so, does it still exist? If a hoax, who created the MJ-12 documents? Were the MJ-12 documents a product of a government disinformation campaign? The answers to these questions may help explain why Congress is having so much trouble getting answers about UAP from the Pentagon and intelligence community.

The original MJ-12 document is an alleged briefing paper for incoming President Dwight D. Eisenhower. Several other documents appeared over time that either were supposed to be MJ-12 internal operating manuals or classified documents that reference Majestic Twelve. Except for one document found at the National Archives, the rest were anonymously sent to people close to the UFO research community. Each new batch ignited debates that distracted UFO researchers and divided them into warring camps. This fight gave ammunition to skeptics about the MJ-12 documents and, by extension, general UFO research. Citing an Air Force investigation, the FBI has dramatically labeled the MJ-12 documents "bogus." The National Archives and Records Administration (NARA) has a detailed disclaimer on their website that disputes their authenticity. As a result of the intrigue, most interested bystanders simply moved on to other topics.

NARA, the FBI, and Air Force each claim the documents are fakes. In the past, these declarations would be enough to put the inquiry to rest. However, with the adoption of historical UAP study provisions, the question becomes, assuming these documents are fakes, who faked them? If it is shown to be a UFO researcher, the story quickly comes to an end. However, in the declassified record, there is no evidence of a privately created hoax, only inferences. There is evidence of a hoax, but there was never an official FBI investigation. The lack of any timely investigative follow-up casts doubt on such accusations. On the other hand, based on declassified records, there are many instances of questionable conduct surrounding the UFO/UAP mystery, indicating a probable pattern designed to mislead the public. These documented instances make an organized "debunking" effort appear more plausible. At a minimum, the declassified record provides enough information to make the matter worthy of investigation.

With regard to the specifics of the NARA MJ-12 determination, there are 10 questions raised about a potential confirming document. The document was a purported memorandum from Robert Cutler, President Eisenhower's national security advisor, sent to White House meeting attendees, including General Nathan Twining, about rescheduling an MJ-12 discussion. The memorandum, generally referred to as the "Cutler-Twining memo," listed MJ-12 as a meeting topic, which would provide support of the existence of the program.

For each of 10 specific NARA arguments against the authenticity of the Cutler-Twining memo, there are countervailing arguments that were contemporaneously raised. None are addressed on the NARA website. For instance, the response to the sixth question explains there was no watermark on the Cutler-Twining memo that should be found on White House stationery.

Despite the NARA claim, the late UFO researcher, Stanton Freidman, wrote that the Cutler-Twining memo did contain a watermark which identified it as paper in government use at the time, but not available to the public. There is no evidence that the FBI, or any agency, contacted Mr. Freidman about his evidence before the NARA determination was made. Yet, Freidman was potentially implicated as a participant in a hoax, since he worked with the researchers who found the Cutler-Twining memo.

Assuming the National Archives did not destroy the Cutler-Twining memo, a simple check could be performed to see if it has the watermark claimed by UFO researchers. Since NARA claims the document is a hoax, it should have been preserved as evidence of a criminal breach in Archives security.

Another major point raised in the NARA analysis was that the Cutler-Twining memo was in a newly declassified document box that did not contain any similar documents. This issue was also raised in Stanton Friedman's book. Freidman questioned how the Cutler-Twining memo came to be loosely placed in Box 267. The UFO researcher's decision to review the documents in Box 267 was the result of seemingly unrelated incidents. First, the national archives alerted Friedman that a new batch of Air Force intelligence files were available. Air Force intelligence files were the type of documents that might discuss UFO issues. Second, around the same time, Freidman's research partners received postcards from exotic locations, each having an American embassy, around the world urging them to keep looking. As a result, Freidman's partners went to the archives to look at the contents of Box 267 and found the Cutler-Twining memo. It was in a box that did not contain any other related documents and was not in a particular file. Highly unusual. How it got there is still a mystery. One that neither the FBI nor the National Archives ever interviewed any of the UFO researchers who found it. Curious, since they would be either key witnesses or prime suspects about placement of the memo in a secure government archive. If the document had been placed in Box 267 by a UFO researcher, it would have been a federal crime to create a fake official document and for smuggling it into a secure government archive, breaching NARA security protocols. Yet, no criminal investigation was ever conducted. Considering the effort used to "debunk" the documents, why was there no federal effort made to determine who did it?

NARA's final point on the Cutler-Twining memo was that Robert Cutler was out of the country when the memo was issued.

The Stanton Friedman book counters that there were several examples of procedural memos, like this memo (i.e., changes in meeting dates or times), that were routinely sent out by Mr. Cutler's assistant when he was out of the office.

This saga began when photos of the alleged Eisenhower briefing document were mailed to a person with ties to the UFO research community. Over the years, other purported MJ-12 documents were sent anonymously to UFO researchers. Each had appeared genuine on their face, but deviations from normal documentary procedures have been noted by other UFO researchers in each. The Cutler-Twining memo, the only supporting document found in the National Archives itself, has serious questions of how it got in an unrelated document box requested by a UFO researcher after a suggestion by a NARA employee. In addition to receiving a photographic copy of the first MJ-12 document sent anonymously through the mail, they received postcards from exotic locations, urging them to continue their search.

Even though the FBI received information about the documents, they never took any steps to determine how the Cutler-Twining memo ended up in the National Archives. The FBI website states that they relied upon an Air Force investigation to determine the memo was a hoax. The main goals of the NARA and Air Force investigations were to show that the MJ-12 documents were not government documents. Instead, the three government websites leave the strong implication that UFO researchers faked the documents without any due diligence into how the UFO researchers bypassed the National Archives security process.

Sneaking a document into secure archives is as difficult as sneaking one out. Government officials, including a former national security advisor, have been prosecuted for violating the security protocols of the National Archives. As is well known from today's headlines, the Justice Department takes breaches of classified document procedures very seriously. Yet, in this instance, the FBI did not investigate the matter. It declared the documents "bogus" based on an Air Force investigation. A curious decision for a law enforcement agency. Especially for a document that raises questions about the foundations of government national security policy and National Archive security.

Blaming UFO researchers without any follow-up investigation is consistent with other Air Force, IC, and FBI actions taken in response to interest in the UFO phenomenon. Law enforcement has tended to shy away from these matters when UFO/UAP are the issue. Normal lines of authority tend to blur. Records show non-involved agencies may protect themselves but seldom challenge the authority of an agency that has apparent responsibility for UAP matters. Since September 1947, the FBI was to be kept informed about UFO information but publicly claimed it would not get involved in the subject matter. Given the history of Air Force declarations about UFOs, it is perplexing why the FBI deferred a law enforcement function to the Air Force in the MJ-12 matter.

The Cutler-Twining memo controversy occurred in the 1980s. It displays many earmarks of a disinformation campaign. Just assuming it was a privately generated hoax, considering what the declassified record shows, does a disservice to us all. Congress has adopted mandatory study requirements for the history of UAP policy including possible disinformation efforts. To date, little has been done to investigate these issues, with AARO being underfunded by the DoD. Further, it should not be limited to witnesses who voluntarily come forward as AARO has done. Only a proactive approach will help us find answers. There is enough in the declassified record to support a serious effort to learn from the past about how our government handled these issues.

Overall, use of a coordinated psychological warfare campaign is a distinct probability. Many declassified records show common tactics used to depress interest in the subject. Destruction of quality photos and outright theft were used to keep quality evidence away from the public. Other tactics show a common plan to keep involvement of the intelligence community secret from Congress and the public. Regulations were used to keep trained observers from talking to the media. Regulations intended to eliminate quality witnesses and evidence left the Air Force as the only authoritative source on the subject. The marginalization efforts kept academic institutions from considering the field worthy of study. The debunking recommendations have successfully contributed to today's UAP stigma. This furthers the goal of delay and, if history is a guide, the eventual depression of UAP interest as other policy concerns take center stage.

The examples used in this chapter are not an assortment of random occurrences that led to unintended consequences. During every period of post-WWII history, new methods were deployed to stifle interest. When technology posed new challenges, the tactics changed to meet the new circumstances. As technology helps in one area, it creates other problems for the debunking program. With the rise of the internet, more resources are used to police government websites for inadvertent disclosures. Examples discussed herein show the ability to quickly remove information, which shows that the official narrative is not the whole story.

In the 1950s, pilots were a trusted source of information about what was in our airspace. Air travel was becoming affordable, and more people took to the air. People trusted the profession and early air travel depended on that trust. Publicly accusing a pilot of misidentifying a UFO might eliminate a sighting case, but it would ground a pilot and generally cast doubt about the safety of air travel. The tactics used to denigrate a UFO photo could not be used against professional pilots. The damage caused to the accused pilot and the industry as a whole could risk undermining the entire "debunking" program. Another way was needed to eliminate UFO pilot reports. Even though civilian air safety was the responsibility of the CAA, now FAA, the Air Force stepped in and adopted joint military reporting requirements which applied to civilian pilots.

The Air Force preempted the agency statutorily responsible for civilian air safety for an issue that officially was not a threat to national security. The policy set by regulation (JNAP-146) gave the Air Force a method to suppress pilot speech without facing individual challenges where pilots would lose their flight privileges for speaking out about UFO air safety issues. Using the same method applied to UFO photographers would increase the odds of a nasty pushback from a pilot who lost his livelihood for speaking out. The adopted regulations kept pilots from taking a career-ending risk. It was safer to not officially report a UFO sighting or talk to the press. JNAP-146 stopped these reports before they happened. This regulation gave the Air Force what it wanted with little effort or risk.

Using different approaches to the various "problems" that arose helped the Air Force and CIA implement "debunking" in an efficient manner. As long as Congress could be kept out of the loop, these policies could go on for decades. There was no need for a KGB-style, massive intelligence-gathering footprint to suppress UFO information. AFOSI, using local base intelligence officers to chase down leads, worked remarkably well. At least until 1986, the CIA helped chase down and retrieve government evidence, like radar tapes, that could raise serious questions about the official UFO policy.

The examples used in this book show how determined effort and a few outward policy changes could keep a lid on the flying saucer phenomenon. Tying aspects of the phenomenon to our Cold War struggles helped keep congressional scrutiny at bay. By relying on the trust in the military built up during WWII, these actors could dispose of quality evidence from a small group of Americans who had nothing in common, except they had a camera ready when a UFO happened by. The CIA gathered other documentary evidence held by government officials that might create problems. While this method led to many disgruntled personnel, there was little that could be done with non-disclosure agreements isolating these government workers from each other.

These tactics worked to keep a disparate group of people apart who only shared one common trait. Each had either seen or documented UFO sightings that were more than just "lights in the sky." The "debunking" aspect of the hidden UFO program kept the phenomenon from becoming a public policy topic. As time went by, this strategy began to show flaws.

While the Viet Nam War and Watergate were beginning to erode trust in the government, the Air Force was able to extricate itself from the public study of UFOs. The University of Colorado "Condon" Committee study gave the Air Force an excuse to get rid of Project Blue Book. This move lowered the number of cases where the Air Force had to come up with implausible explanations to discount sightings. Later, in the 1990s, the Air Force was able to tamp down questions about the Roswell crash with the production of two reports costing approximately $40 million dollars.

As the 21st century began, Senate Majority Leader Harry Reid was able to slip a small expenditure into the DoD budget to study UAP. Simultaneously, improved sensors were able to better see unusual objects that concerned naval aviators. When a pilot could take a picture of a UAP with her cell phone, it made it harder for the CIA or another intelligence agency to scoop up radar tapes and be done with it. Despite the stigma, pilots, normally a close-knit group, discussed incidents among themselves. Eventually, these concerns reached Congress, mostly through the efforts of the short-lived AATIP program.

Current challenges were harder to contain than when the CIA and Air Force used a variety of illegal tactics to brush aside Dr. Leon

Davidson's justified concerns.[201] With the Navy willing to look into its pilot concerns that the Air Force would not, members of the Intelligence and Armed Services Committees began to take notice. This time, the DoD/IC pushback no longer had its usual success. The Navy's UAP Task Force led to a 2021 report to Congress, which broke from past policies. While national security committees began hearing from Navy aviators in classified settings, it gave them a view of what had been kept from Congress for decades.

The psychological warfare tactics that had been so successful for generations could no longer quell the inquiries from Congress. Now, Congress has adopted multiple rounds of mandatory study requirements. This mandated study includes "any efforts to obfuscate, manipulate public opinion, hide, or otherwise provide incorrect unclassified or classified information about unidentified anomalous phenomena or related activities."[202] Even before this study is complete, the declassified records already show improper activities that justify the inquiry. It is becoming clearer that the UFO/UAP mystery hides more than just objects. Evidence shows it hides a long-term program meant to keep this issue from Congress through the use of psychological warfare.

---

[201] Despite all of the inaccuracies of the "CIA's Role in the Study of UFOs, 1947–90," it is still prominently featured on the current CIA archive website. See, https://www.cia.gov/static/cia-role-study-UFOs.pdf.

[202] 50 U.S.C. §3373(j)(1)(B)(ii)(III).

CHAPTER NINETEEN

FINAL THOUGHTS: WHY ALL THE EFFORT?

The UAP dilemma raises two serious concerns. First, there are physical craft exhibiting impossible flight characteristics. How serious these concerns are to national security is still an open question. Second, the puzzling reaction of our military and intelligence communities to congressional concerns raises the probability that our elected officials are not in control. In a democracy, it is hard to determine which problem is more serious. A potential national security threat or that long-term military/intelligence policy decisions are being made without the knowledge of our civilian representatives. Both have serious ramifications, which united political parties into a unique political consensus during a time of disunity. However, considering recent political developments, there is a serious question as to whether this UAP bipartisanship will last.

Historically, the declassified record shows activities aimed at depressing interest in the UAP/UFO mystery. It would be difficult to claim that all of these declassified incidents have innocent explanations. Are these declassified instances only the tip of the iceberg? Also, does this past still influence today's response to UAP? This book has discussed the many commonalities between past polices and today's response. There are parallels that strongly suggest past military/intelligence policies are still controlling our current actions.

Since the 1948 decision by the Air Force chief of staff to eliminate any consideration of a possible non-terrestrial source of

UAP, the government has held fast to this posture. This decision to eliminate consideration of one potential source of the phenomenon was bolstered by the conclusions of the Robertson Panel. Today, Congress is still hearing the same answers from a bureaucracy relying on these past assumptions.

This leaves us at virtually the same place we occupied in 1953. They aren't ours. They aren't foreign adversaries. Yet, if real, they can't be from any other source. Even unknown cases are not worrisome if we had enough data. Reducing the number of unknowns through a variety of means is how to eliminate the problem. As long as our batting average of solving cases gets high enough, we don't need to worry about the remaining unknown cases. These assumptions have been made for decades and are still used by AARO. Thanks to the UAPTF, the biggest difference today is that UAP are considered to be of scientific interest. In 1953, the distinguished scientific panel saw no scientific value in the study of UFOs. Despite this significant change, we are not approaching the phenomenon any differently than in 1953. Yet, the phenomenon keeps posing problems that will not go away.

Since World War II Foo Fighters shadowed planes in both the European and Pacific theaters, the fascination of UAP with military assets, especially nuclear facilities, has continued to this day. With our sophisticated sensors, today's military has been able to gather more quality data about UAP. Yet, despite these advancements, we are still looking for answers the way we did in the flying saucer era.

Embarrassment alone cannot explain this behavior, even if the representative examples in this book are the only incidents. There must be something more that would cause the destruction of private property, slanderous accusations, and the prevention of air safety investigations. The most simple explanation, if one accepts the UAP testimony of Navy pilots, is that the military cannot prevent UAP intrusions into our airspace. Since they cannot control the comings and goings of these craft, the Air Force/IC have tried to keep this inadequacy from Congress and the public. Even if we can't control the phenomenon, shouldn't we try to duplicate it?

Apparently, our decades of trying to duplicate it have not resulted in a breakthrough. If it had, we would have flying saucers in our military. The Senate Intel Committee believes there are classified programs still trying for a breakthrough that will not grant access to properly cleared elected officials. One must assume that the intelligence committees have information that justifies a multi-year legislative quest. Given the continued "stigma" around the phenomenon, experienced political leaders would not risk pushing this legislation without evidence. Since we cannot see their classified inquiries, their bipartisanship shows no disagreement over the merits of this assumption.

The DoD/IC behavior alone makes it unlikely that core UAP are a man-made phenomenon. While every defense-oriented media outlet covers the ups and downs of the hypersonic missile race or artificial intelligence application to the battlefield, UAP do not raise the same DoD urgency as these other cutting-edge research problems. Instead, Congress is concerned about UAP while the DoD/IC are not.

The lack of concern, however, does not translate into the same kind of DoD/IC behavior when it comes to access of deeply buried programs. Congress has tried a variety of methods to obtain access. They seek information in classified settings from whistleblowers and propose multiple rounds of legislation to gain access. All that AARO can say in response is that they haven't "**yet**" found any of these programs. But they attack efforts of a congressional subcommittee to conduct oversight into the issue. At the same time, past behavior denigrating those who believe there is more behind the curtain continues. Some of this conduct comes from AARO, which was authorized to find the answers.

If UAP are what former Navy pilots Ryan Graves and David Fravor believe they are, it would be illogical for the DoD/IC to just ignore the "problem." Instead, the national security apparatus should be actively working to figure out how UAP operate. If there are UAP that we have no defense against, wouldn't we try to develop one?

If real, we would be racing to develop our own similar platforms before any other terrestrial adversary gets there first. From outward behavior, it is apparent that we have not achieved any significant breakthroughs having practical applications. Therefore, those attempting to reverse engineer a UAP have been keeping the secret to protect their monopoly from congressional oversight. Once Congress has knowledge of these programs, they would naturally seek to control the expenditures, method, and manner of research. Having been handed the potentially most lucrative assignment in defense contracting history, those in exclusive possession of exotic UAP materials would be doing everything they can to keep their monopoly.

While Congress is pursuing these secret monopolies, defense contractors and in-house programs appear to be taking steps to protect their investment. In addition to the upside of keeping hold of a valuable contract, they would have an incentive to hide their past work from congressional scrutiny. Often, programs with little or no supervision tend to take shortcuts. For example, Area 51 has had secret weapons development programs that were found to use environmentally risky methods.[203] The clandestine use and improper disposal of hazardous materials in advanced defense research has occurred in the past. Improper past practices would be a further reason to cover up these programs. In addition to losing these valuable contracts, each party could be responsible for environmental cleanup costs. With Congress aggressively pursuing these hidden programs, these improper practices are likely

---

[203] *i.e.* https://lasvegassun.com/news/1996/aug/08/feds-investigating-burning-of-hazardous-waste-at-a/.

accelerating as they try to achieve breakthroughs before they lose their monopoly.

Due to the twin concerns of the threat potential of UAP and the inadequate response by the DoD/IC, Congress has been pro-active in its legislative approach to the subject. When the Senate Intelligence Committee released the FY2023 Intelligence Authorization Act, the committee comments by Chair Senator Mark Warner (D-VA) lamented the DoD lack of cooperation and called on UAP reports to be limited as follows:

> "Temporary nonattributed objects, or those that are positively identified as man-made after analysis, will be passed to appropriate offices and should not be considered under the definition as unidentified aerospace-undersea phenomena."[204]

This statement sums up the different approaches of the congressional national security committees and the DoD/IC. Congress wants identified objects to be part of the normal DoD identification process, while AARO should focus on core UAP that cannot be attributed to a particular source. Instead, AARO considers any object that was not instantly identified to be a UAP. This keeps balloons, traditional drones, clutter and other identified objects under AARO's control so they can include them in public reports to Congress. This focuses the public's attention on AARO's "batting average" of solved cases. However, if you strip away cases that have a conventional profile, you are left with only core UAP cases. These core cases are the type of objects seen by former Navy pilots like David Fravor, Alex Dietrich, and Ryan Graves. AARO should have more resources devoted to their analysis. At present, the DoD and IC claim to have no evidence that these anomalous

---

[204] Report 117–132: Intelligence Authorization Act for Fiscal Year 2023, Report together with Additional Views, Senate Select Committee on Intelligence, July 22, 2022.

craft are tied to any terrestrial source. It makes no sense, except for public relations purposes, for AARO to continue to count mundane objects as UAP. It obscures the truly anomalous sightings and drains resources from their analysis.

In July 2022, the Intelligence Community Inspector General passed along to the Senate and the House Committees on Intelligence a whistleblower complaint that was filed by David Grusch. He is a former Air Force, National Geospatial-Intelligence Agency (NGA), and National Reconnaissance Office (NRO) intelligence officer. Grusch was detailed by NGA to the UAP Task Force from 2019 to 2021 where he had clearances "canceled, delayed, denied, and/or improperly obstructed." These actions were taken in retaliation for his inquiries into hidden UAP programs. When this complaint of reprisal was forwarded to the House and Senate Intel Committees, the Inspector General determined that the complaint was "credible" and "urgent." After receiving this information, the Senate Intel Committee determined there was a need to act on the complaint of reprisal and likely followed up with further investigatory steps. Their response to the information they recovered was a unanimous referral to the Senate for legislation seeking to expose these alleged secret programs to normal congressional oversight.

As this struggle between Congress and the DoD/IC continues, we are seeing more evidence of the type of delaying and debunking tactics reminiscent of the flying saucer/UFO eras. In 1952, the CIA and Air Force delayed Truman's requested UFO investigation until a more friendly Eisenhower Administration could take over. Once its recommendations were approved by the 1953 scientific panel, the CIA circulated different versions of the Panel's recommendations so it could hide the domestic "debunking" plan from many elements of the Administration. Going forward, the plan was to keep information a closely held secret. Even before the results of the Robertson Panel were circulated outside of the CIA, implementation measures were started to prevent scientists and engineers from studying the mystery. By 1958, the CIA was also able to derail a sincere effort to inform Congress about the CIA debunking policies.

Simultaneously, the Air Force began its portion of the "debunking" policy. Airlines were told to keep their pilots from talking to the press about UFO sightings. An Air Force mandatory UFO sighting report policy began preventing civilian pilots from speaking about sightings without first filing a report with the Air Force. Civilian air safety regulators were excluded from this process. Local Air Force intelligence officers misappropriated quality UFO photographs and destroyed them. People who complained were either ignored or branded hoaxsters.

As time went by, the tactics were adjusted to take on new challenges. With technological changes, quality photographs were not sought. The fact that many UFOs are being photoshopped helped the Air Force do its job. Instead, government websites were scrubbed of UAP-related information where the public could sometimes learn about actual government interest. Other incidents discussed herein showed that the CIA continued to be involved in squelching information long after it publicly claimed disinterest.

Today, significant elements of the defense/intelligence world continue to be involved while still keeping Congress uninformed. When the Navy formed the UAPTF to address repeated aviator concerns, the Air Force continued its policy of keeping its pilots and nuclear launch officers in the dark about Air Force/UAP activities. The Air Force did little to contribute to the *Preliminary Assessment* prepared for Congress. The CIA refused to participate at all. CIA noninvolvement continues through the reporting period of the 2023 annual report, which documents Agency lack of participation. A statutory requirement for IC assistance of the UAP program continues to be ignored.

Besides noninvolvement by key players, active debunking still continues. When two whistleblowers stepped forward, the DoD denied both Luis Elizondo and David Grusch were associated with UAP programs even though both were. David Grusch had his medical records leaked about PTSD treatment he received for his decorated service in an active combat zone. Throughout this time period, the DoD professes transparency while returning to the policy of not releasing UAP videos. Even after the 2017 declassification of the FLIR, Gimbal, and GOFAST naval aviation videos, the Pentagon refused to make them available to researchers until April 2020. At a time when high-quality color videos of drone footage of Chinese and Russian harassment are immediately released, the DoD fights release of black and white, grainy UAP videos. All the while, Congress is denied access to top secret programs that work on UAP issues.

In sum, while the tactics have changed to meet new challenges, the "debunking" program is still alive and well. The 2021 Navy UAP Task Force *Preliminary Assessment* warned Congress that the "stigma" surrounding UAP continued to hamper progress. After UAP authority was passed from the Navy's UAPTF to DoD's AARO, even incremental forward progress has either slowed or stopped. This is despite successive rounds of ever-tightening legislation. The latest 2023 annual report does announce some procedural progress, but the AARO emphasis is still on mundane objects despite repeated congressional requests to focus on concerning phenomenon. Now, Congress is poised to take much of the responsibility out of the hands of the DoD/IC and pursue an alternative strategy.

In 2023, in addition to requiring the DoD to fully fund AARO, Congress seeks to take away some of the tools the DoD/IC use to hold up progress. Stripping clandestine UAP programs of their funding will encourage UAP research programs to inform proper congressional committees about their work. This punitive measure will also affect other projects that have been used as conduits to fund the hidden programs. If this method of funding is continued after the notification deadline, the transfers, even if legal before, would become a fraud upon the government. This could result in criminal penalties as well as procurement remedies, including debarment of the contractor, i.e. prohibited from contracting with the federal government.

The defunding of non-reporting programs is a proposal intended to allow Congress to regain control of its expenditures. It may also lead to information that helps explain the sources and capabilities of UAP. The AARO search for the sources of UAP could, in many ways, become moot. Also, the release of UAP records legislation should further add to our understanding of the history of government UAP studies.

At present, AARO acknowledges having records of UAP activities back to 1996, over 27 years ago. Under this independent oversight approach, records older than 25 years would be presumed to be declassified. Records discussing and photographs showing UAP from the 1940s through 1998 should put to rest the notion that UAP are a recent phenomenon. In addition to changing how we view this potential threat; it would also raise questions as to when these "off the books" programs started.

The records declassification procedures would allow others besides AARO to be part of the process. Academic institutions, think tanks, private researchers and citizens could all contribute. AARO waiting for peer review of its conclusions based on only current data would no longer be the only option. The laws before Congress for FY2024 are another step in the determined effort of the core committees to understand UAP. Unless it is derailed in the chaos over keeping the government running, these bills should pass. Yet, there are already indications that a small number in Congress, acting on behalf of entrenched interests, are trying to delay, weaken, or to prevent implementation of the FY2024 UAP legislative proposals.[205] Only time will tell if the progress has stopped.

What they will find is hard to tell, but there have been indicators. First of all, the scope of this "off the books" government is probably not as large as some people claim. Records discussed from the Robertson Panel time period show the great lengths the CIA and Air Force went to keep other military branches and agencies out of the loop. Even within the Air Force and CIA, these efforts were confined to specific departments. In the Air Force, the Air Technical Intelligence Center (ATIC) at Wright-Patterson Air Force Base in Dayton, Ohio was the location of the Air Force's Project Blue Book. ATIC was also home to laboratories that assessed foreign technology. While perhaps not the only place, it would have been the most logical place for the Air Force to assess UAP, the ultimate foreign technology. There may be earmarks of secret UAP programs at Wright-Patterson AFB such as unusual levels of contamination resulting from a largely unregulated program studying exotic and possibly dangerous materials.

The Air Force's intelligence arm is likely to be another element of the secret program. Project Blue Book relied upon the Air Force Office of Special Investigations (AFOSI) to do most of its field work. AFOSI had both law enforcement and counterintelligence authority. Among other cases, AFOSI was implicated in the 1960 Joseph Perry missing UFO photo incident, according to the FBI. With ATIC and AFOSI having classified duties involving foreign materials analysis and law enforcement/counterintelligence responsibilities, their personnel would routinely work on highly classified matters. The most likely places to look for hidden UAP-related programs. The dual law enforcement/intelligence function of AFOSI could help keep the UFO/UAP hidden programs secret.

---

[205] https://thedebrief.org/uap-disclosure-act-receives-pushback-from-lawmakers-on-capitol-hill-as-bipartisan-fight-for-transparency-continues/.

Non-disclosure agreements, required by AFOSI and used for witnesses to UFO/UAP activity would help keep these incidents secret. Both ATIC and AFOSI records would be a good place to start an inquiry into past and present UAP programs.

The CIA is also likely to use the same methods to closely contain knowledge of its involvement in the UFO/UAP issue. Declassified evidence and the statements of John Callahan, the FAA Division Chief of the Accidents and Investigations branch, indicate that the CIA Office of Scientific Intelligence (OSI) was involved in the UFO issue from 1952 until at least 1986, contradicting the 1990 official history about the length of CIA UFO involvement. The CIA's OSI was the center of other illegal programs during the early UFO era, so it is unsurprising that they would be tasked with clandestine UFO-related duties. However, since 1954, other intelligence agencies have been added to the mix. Many of these agencies arose out of the need for satellite surveillance and signals intelligence. Segments of these highly secret programs would likely become part of the UAP clandestine network. Each is now subject to oversight by the House and Senate Intelligence Committees.

The FBI also poses questions about the extent of its involvement in any long-term UAP program. According to the 1970s Church Committee and many other sources, it was at the center of many legally questionable activities, dating back to the 1930s. FBI involvement was publicly acknowledged in 1949 by the final report of Project Sign. Its agents conducted "investigations of the character and reliability of witnesses of incidents and by providing other investigative services."[206]

It also instigated the first overt activity after the Robertson Panel issued its recommendations. As part of a briefing for the CIA

---

[206] https://archive.org/details/ProjectSIGN/mode/2up. Unidentified Aerial Objects: Project Sign, technical report no. F-TR-2274-IA, @ p. 3 (12 of 72).

Office of National Estimates (ONE), FBI Director J. Edgar Hoover learned of the "debunking" program. Immediately thereafter, an FBI agent met with CSI-LA member Dr. Walther Reidel and dissuaded him from continuing his private research into the phenomenon. Since the CIA had yet to formally circulate the Panel's recommendations to other agencies, the timing of events demonstrates that Hoover was the most likely suspect to have ordered the contact.

At the time, there were FBI agents tasked from its D.C. headquarters to Los Angeles for House of Representatives on Un-American Activities hearings being conducted at the same time. One could easily be redirected to North American Aviation to contact Reidel and quickly report back to CIA OSI by February 9, 1953. The declassified report is in the CIA's files, but not in the FBI archives. FBI declassified records about UFOs seem to have one thing in common: Director Hoover was the sole recipient of these reports. He was front and center in the Joseph Perry incident, solely for the purpose of keeping the FBI away from blame over Perry's missing UFO photograph. In the same batch of unclassified records of 1960 FBI involvement, there was a report by an agent who attended a UFO meeting. The memo showed no apparent law enforcement purpose and was sent only to Hoover. From other sparse records available about FBI/UFO connections, Director Hoover is apparently the only recipient. Perhaps FBI involvement was a closely held prerogative of the Director. This would mimic many other forays by the FBI into extralegal activities against dissidents like the Rev. Martin Luther King and Viet Nam War protestors.

Hiding classified programs would be easier in agencies that are already involved with highly classified work. While there may be a spiderweb of UAP-related programs throughout the IC, the scope of the secrecy of UAP research and potential active measures could still maintain a smaller footprint than would be expected. Recent actions indicate that hidden UAP programs are probably not a vast, deep state conspiracy involving other subjects. While many will doubt the existence of a secret UAP infrastructure hidden from Congress, the strong bipartisan support in the Senate Select Committee on Intelligence for proposed legislation indicates otherwise. Just the act of proposing this independent oversight bill means that the Senate Intel Committee has learned enough information to believe that such programs exist. The mere act of proposing this legislation is a startling admission of the Committee's lack of program oversight.

In trying to determine the scope of this program, there are some current indicators. After the initial AATIP program ran its course, DoD intelligence agent Luis Elizondo went through the declassification procedure to have the Defense Intelligence Agency (DIA) declassify the FLIR, Gimbal, and GOFAST naval aviation videos. Elizondo was able to get them declassified in August 2017 and, post-retirement, published by *Politico* and the *New York Times*. It was plainly obvious from media reports in the aftermath of their release that the rest of the DoD, IC, and Trump Administration were caught unawares. It took until April 2020 for the Pentagon to grant FOIA records requests for copies of what could easily be found on the internet. The release of the videos and later pushback shows the DoD/IC are not speaking with one voice.

This lack of coordination continued. With the June 25, 2021 release of the Navy UAP Task Force's *Preliminary Assessment: Unidentified Aerial Phenomena*, many official UAP policies were called into question. For the first time since the 1953 Robertson Panel, UAP were considered to be of scientific interest. Most of the sightings were seen visually by highly trained personnel and captured by a wide array of sensors. In the past, often after contrary statements were recanted, the official position was that sensor data did not capture the objects spotted by eyewitnesses. These eyewitness/sensor incidents caused the UAPTF to state that the objects were "probably" real, physical objects. This admission was a far cry from the official policy that, given enough information, all

UFO sightings are a (1) mistake, a (2) delusion, or an (3) outright fabrication. Also, the UAPTF found that 11 of the 143 unknown objects caused near misses of our aircraft. This meant that the objects were either a safety hazard or part of a threat to national security. Previous DoD statements have consistently claimed that there has never been a UFO report that threatened national security. The Navy UAP Task Force, while making only incremental advancements, was at odds with prevailing DoD/IC UAP policies. Much like the 1952-53 Naval Photo Interpretation Laboratory and the CIA/Air Force/Robertson Panel coming to different conclusions on two high-quality UFO films.

The Navy/Air Force difference from DoD continued with AARO. In 2022, AARO was formed as the UAPTF disbanded, putting the Pentagon in control of UAP study. While AARO started with claims of transparency, the UAPTF beginnings of openness began to recede. Videos like the three released in 2017 are no longer available to prevent disclosure of sources and methods. While the Biden Administration accelerated releases of high-quality, color video footage of confrontations with the Russians and Chinese, AARO was severely restricting UAP footage. The short-lived era of transparency seems to have come to an end. Because of budget limitations, AARO delegated its historical review to the Air Force, which still clings to the historic UFO position. In other words, the service branch being investigated will also play a role in investigating itself. These ebbs and flows of transparency show that there is not a large, monolithic program. Rather, different elements of a large organization working at cross purposes.

The harsh reaction of the AARO Director Sean Kirkpatrick to congressional whistleblower testimony makes one question whether AARO is the proper vehicle to get to the bottom of this mystery. With the DoD/IC history of being less than candid about its UFO studies, one wonders whether AARO is helping these factions delay UAP information to Congress. If there is truly a split within DoD and the IC, AARO, at a minimum, is caught right in the middle of this tug of war. Today's difference is that those who want more transparency about UAP have Congress on their side. In the past, there was no support for personnel who chafed at the illogical restrictions against discussing potential safety/national security concerns. There was no recourse for even high-ranking officers who witnessed a UFO. If required to sign a non-disclosure agreement or ordered not to talk about it, there was no outlet to protest.

The Whistleblower Protection Act of 1989[207] was not available for most of the Flying Saucer/UFO Era. Even after its adoption, it would be a risky step to take without any potential allies available. Most either kept quiet or just retired out of frustration. It is only today that the "stigma" has reduced enough, largely due to congressional interest, for a few personnel to consider speaking out about UAP. For this reason, the vast majority of those coming forward appear to be retired military/intelligence witnesses. They now have the beginnings of a support system in place to protect their speech. The adoption of specific whistleblower protections by Congress makes it safer, but the secret UAP infrastructure still has enough influence for its adherents to close ranks and continue their mostly anonymous challenges. The question is for how long? While we are in the third consecutive round of stricter UAP legislative standards, it is becoming clearer that Congress is not giving up.

Except for the primary players (i.e. Air Force, CIA, and probably other IC elements), the idea of a vast, coordinated "deep state" looks unlikely. Instead, there are probably disparate siloed special access programs scattered throughout government, possibly unaware of each other. This will make them difficult to track down without the help of personnel coming forward. It will also be hard for congressional inquiries to track them down without resorting to financial (budgetary) persuasion. Tracking funding will take time, especially in an organization riddled with "need to know" access

---

[207] 5 U.S.C. §2302(b)(8)-(9).

limitations. This process, even with the passage of the pending legislation, could take years.

The dilemma with the DoD/IC is complicated by the disfunction occurring in the House of Representatives. As this book was going to print, the government was running on a short-term continuing resolution and none of the regular appropriations bills had been agreed to by the House and Senate. The Speaker of the House remained a contested office, with many roadblocks preventing any budget deal, let alone approval of pending UAP legislation. As in 1968, when a UFO congressional hearing was overshadowed by other events, the bipartisan approach to this subject may be overshadowed by just keeping the government functioning. Delaying legislative approvals until the second session of the 118th Congress (2024) pushes these issues to a presidential election year. With formal UAP reporting requirements expiring at the end of 2026, the DOD/IC delaying strategy may be working to their advantage. Hopefully, for the sake of many important issues, including UAP, the two parties can resolve seemingly intractable differences and return to regular order.

As before, the UAP phenomenon may not be able to overcome these obstacles. Yet, this phenomenon may be the type of issue that can rise above the increasingly partisan mood of Congress and the nation. If so, looking at the phenomenon itself, the need to address the UAP issues seems to have many reasons for this continuing cooperation. Partisan rancor aside, no matter the source of these physical objects, terrestrial or non-terrestrial, they could be existential threats. Throwing aside bipartisanship will not help us address these possible threats.

If core, high performance UAP are of terrestrial origin, it could mean that another country has developed weapons platforms for which we may have no defense. Even if it is an ally or a non-aligned country, it would still be a destabilizing development. The risk would be that the secrets would not stay in friendly hands. Also, if one country made a breakthrough, why couldn't an adversary make the same breakthrough? The current state of our own UAP research would instantly become a primary national priority. One that needs the immediate attention of Congress and the Administration. One where Congress needs to find out if segments of the DoD and IC already know some of the answers but are not telling our elected civilian leadership. Without knowing the current status of efforts to acquire the same technology, it will be hard for Congress to set national policy to counter any potential terrestrial threat.

If evidence points to non-terrestrial sources, the sooner that Congress learns of it, the better. This revelation will have the most profound implications. Do these craft have weapon capabilities? What do we know about the sources of UAP? How do we address what we learn? How do we reveal this information to the public? Congress needs to be involved in each of these issues. It is difficult to plan when you do not know why you are planning. Staying uninformed could lead to disclosures from other sources that may not have our best interests in mind. There are also many other ways that this knowledge could become public. Inadvertent disclosure, disclosure by an adversary, or disclosure by the UAP sources themselves, could lead to people losing even more faith in our elected leaders. Congress, with its bipartisan approach, has the best chance of disclosing this information in a way that will be accepted by a solid majority of the public.

If Congress does not act in a proactive manner, there are ways our technical resources could force the issue. Today, with the deployment of the Webb Telescope and other similar platforms, the discovery of relatively nearby intelligent life is only a matter of time. Refusing to consider this possibility may have been easier in 1948 when the Air Force destroyed all copies of an internal study suggesting this possibility. Today, we face the real possibility that local intelligent civilizations may soon be confirmed through our space-based sensors. After confirmation of life elsewhere, there will be a natural tendency to put more scrutiny on evidence of non-terrestrial visitations/intrusions on Earth. When the next link is made to visitations on this planet, it would further damage the credibility of Congress, the military, and the intelligence community. A failure to consider a non-terrestrial source could go down in history beside scientists who claimed powered flight was impossible in the months before the Wright Brothers took off from Kitty Hawk or late 18th-century French scientists who proclaimed that only peasants saw stones fall from the sky just prior to the 1803 discovery of meteorites. Our failure to consider the possibility of a non-terrestrial source, if its discovery occurs anyway, will damage our already fragile institutions. The question will be: "Why didn't you tell us?"

Passing this "buck" onto future generations risks an uncoordinated disclosure, which will heighten anxiety and risk the rise of Joseph McCarthy-like demigods who exploit the situation. Considering that future administrations will be focusing an increasing amount of their time and effort on climate change and emerging military challenges, the future does not look like a more promising time to wait to announce a non-terrestrial presence.

This is why the history of our military's experience with UAP is so important. What is learned from the history of our UAP interactions can tell us much about their controllers. Overall, non-terrestrial sources of UAP could fall into four general categories: *Hostile, Transactional, Indifferent,* or *Supportive.* We will need to plan for each eventuality. It is probable that the sources of UAP are a mixture of civilizations with a variety of reasons for their presence. Our past interactions will help us determine what we are facing.

Our history can help shape our response to these craft and their controllers. The testimony of our best trained pilots, corroborated with sensor data, already shows that they have the **capability** to do us harm. First, we must determine whether any of the civilizations interacting with us **intend** harm. The length of interactions with them could be a guide to their intent. How long have they exhibited hostile behavior? If we have been interacting with them for 80 years with no overt hostility, it is unlikely that any of the civilizations intend military conquest. One does not wait 80 years for your adversary to become more capable of defending themselves before attacking.

However, there are some disturbing signs. Some pilots have reported that their weapons systems have been disabled during encounters. The same type of conduct has allegedly occurred with our nuclear weapons. When this has occurred, what steps, if any, have UAP taken to press their advantage? The answers to these questions would help us understand what we are dealing with.

Without knowledge of UAP historical actions, it will be difficult for Congress to help determine what policy priorities should be established. A history of military encounters would be a good place to start. Other agencies could also be of immense help. For instance, NASA could provide information of any interference directed at our space program. Are manned space missions being monitored in the same manner as some of our military pilots have claimed? If so, for what purpose? Have UAP interfered with any missions? The current NASA review of unclassified, open-source information will do nothing to provide our elected leaders with answers.

The September 14, 2023 report on NASA's unclassified study merely stated that more work was needed.[208] Interviews with astronauts and mission control personnel, along with review of sensor information, could help determine whether we are facing any civilizations that mean us harm. These steps were not recommended in the NASA report.

---

[208] NASA, *Unidentified Anomalous Phenomena: Independent Study Team Report*, September 14, 2023; Unidentified Anomalous Phenomena: Independent Study Team Report, September 14, 2023.

Considering the length of probable interactions with UAP, the longer it has been occurring, the less likely that any of the civilizations interacting with us are overtly hostile. Yet, overt hostility may not be the only sign of harm being caused to our civilization. Harm could occur in a more subtle fashion. If any of the civilizations see our planet and nearby environs as a resource, their presence could be purely transactional. For instance, since UAP have been encountered underwater, they could be mining our seabed. They may be here to mine polymetallic nodules from the ocean floor. They are abundant and are largely out of our reach. Since UAP have been witnessed performing maneuvers that place tremendous stress on their craft and at least some are submersible, these craft could perform seabed mining. Resources that could be used by us in the future once we gain the technical know-how to safely extract these nodules from the ocean floor.

Another example could be the Moon. The far side of the Moon never faces the Earth. There has never been truly high-resolution photography available to the public of the dark side. This is even though there have been several missions that have surveyed the dark side. The next Artemis mission will orbit the dark side and take high-resolution photographs. If shared with congressional oversight committees without redactions, it could reveal activity. If one or more non-terrestrial civilizations are present, a logical place that they would mine materials to support their local operations would be the far side of the Moon. If the purpose of their presence is purely transactional, intensive mining operations on the dark side of the Moon would be logical, given the level of their technology.[209] Like the seabed, it would be a location that is difficult for our

---

[209] Helium-3 can be used to fuel nuclear fusion. Because the Moon does not have a magnetic field like the Earth, it is an abundant source of Helium-3, deposited via solar winds. Their presence could be intended to harvest H³. https://www.esa.int/Enabling_Support/Preparing_for_the_Future/Space_for_Ear th/Energy/Helium-3_mining_on_the_lunar_surface.

civilization to access. The removal of materials of value, many of which may be more important to us in the future, could be done relatively unhindered.

Transactional motives may not be overtly harmful, but take advantage of our current level of development. In addition to purely commercial motives, another possibility could be observation by an uncaring presence. Near Earth advanced civilizations may not have any empathy or hostility for us. One can't assume that other planetary civilizations have the same emotional makeup as we do. They could simply be indifferent to our plight. If World War II foo fighters are the same craft, from the same sources as UAP, they could be here only to observe. Their initial interest could have been peaked by our development of nuclear weapons. Perhaps they are observing us until we pass this critical stage in our development. Sighting reports did accelerate in the years after WWII. If we do not pass this phase of development, facing both climate change and the threat of nuclear war, they may be monitoring to see if they could take advantage of our failures. If we succeed, they could be here to learn about us as an emerging threat. Any information known about their intentions would help us plan for the future. Letting Congress know what we already know could help us better understand their present intentions.

The history of our interactions with civilizations indifferent to our plight would look much like the behavior we already see. Observation that sometimes interacts with our military assets in a way that shows the futility of our defensive measures. The disabling of weapons systems, including nuclear weapons, demonstrates that, while they do not attack us, they have the capability to defend against any hostile actions we may attempt. This would explain the reticence of DoD, NASA, and the IC to provide any information to Congress. Our military has faced a threat that they cannot defend against and have been trying to play it down. At some point, a civilization in our local group of stars may have even approached this planet's nuclear powers to attempt to dissuade us from continuing down this threatening path. Such knowledge would be valuable as background for any future attempt to open a dialogue with these illusive visitors. Starting diplomatic relations with civilizations that know our joint history, while our diplomats do not, places humanity at a severe disadvantage.

Finally, one or more of the non-terrestrial civilizations could be supportive, but constrained by inter-planetary protocols regarding non-interference. If there is more than one civilization interacting with us, we are unlikely to be the first civilization they have encountered who are at our stage of development. Their non-interference protocols would likely be developed to prevent a nascent society from skipping steps in their development and exporting warlike qualities to other habitable planets. If, from our history, we have already learned that there are civilizations that can aid us, these would be the first that we should attempt to approach. Supportive civilizations could help us understand the protocols that are in use and assist us in understanding the motives of those civilizations that are hostile, uncaring, or merely have a transactional motivation. This information would also help us deal with less friendly non-terrestrial civilizations. We could negotiate with a supportive civilization for technology to help us meet our current planetary challenges. Even if they do not share technology, we could seek guidance about our research and development efforts to learn which are most likely to bear fruit to help us face our planetary challenges. Just the fact they are here indicates that we still have much to learn about their mode of travel. Data captured from our sensors could help provide clues that are known by hidden programs that refuse to share what has been learned with Congress.

Regardless of what we are facing, gathering as much information as possible will help us formulate successful strategies for dealing with these unique challenges. If there are terrestrial or non-terrestrial UAP in our possession as the latest legislative proposal assumes, a rediscovery of past knowledge by Congress will move us to the next phase of UAP study. We will move past the "whether they are real" phase. If UAP are of recent terrestrial design, it will change how we approach diplomacy and probably require a crash industrial program to meet the challenge. If the recovered craft/materials are non-terrestrial, recovered decades ago, an even wider variety of challenges must be addressed. The more knowledge we possess about what we face, the better able we will be to plan our future.

The fact that a unanimous Senate Select Committee on Intelligence added new UAP provisions to the FY2024 Intelligence Authorization Act means that choices must be made very soon. The DoD, IC, NASA, Congress, Biden Administration, and others need to make a choice. Are they going to begin planning for this series of challenges? Or are we going to continue to ignore these emerging issues? If we find out that they are here, we don't need to wait until we figure out for ourselves how they got here.

The DoD, through AARO, has opted for delay. AARO's approach has been to follow historic policies. Working hard to solve mundane cases to improve AARO's "batting average." In the meantime, AARO ignores the testimony of our own pilots and relies on "sensor errors" to eliminate corroborating evidence for these mysterious reports.

The recent personnel changes in AARO management points to further delays. If the delays lead to a further hardening of congressional resolve, the DoD/IC bureaucracy could change tactics. Former AARO Director Sean Kirkpatrick has floated a non-terrestrial possibility that could be an indicator of a revised tactic. He has speculated that the metallic orbs, which have been part of the mystery as far back as WWII, may be pilotless probes. These probes, according to a draft scientific paper, could have been launched by unmanned objects passing through the solar system at sub-light speed. Considering the time it would take sub-light speed objects to arrive here, the threat of the non-terrestrial civilization that launched the probes would be negligible. This tactic, while ignoring the sightings by highly trained pilots of larger objects such as the *Nimitz* "tic-tacs", could satisfy those who do not look closely at the evidence. Clearly, the tactics used to impede congressional efforts are not working. Others may be used to divide the unified support for unfettered UAP study. This "ET-lite" scenario could concede off-world visitations in a less threatening manner, regardless of the other probabilities. It would not explain most sightings, but this theory could be used to stop further inquiries. A Plan "B" for the DoD/IC.

With so many current unknowns, a bipartisan approach is critical. A united front is needed to cope with the bureaucratic headwinds that the core national security committees have faced. In the long run, the answers will not be Republican or Democratic answers. They will be based on what we learn from implementation of the pending UAP legislation. Bipartisanship will also help the American public adjust to this new reality, whatever it entails. As important as finding out what is behind true UAP, explaining it to the public will be vital. It is no coincidence that Senate Majority Leader Schumer (D-NY) teamed up with three Republicans and two Democrats to propose a comprehensive plan to release UFO/UAP records.

The final version of the FY2024 NDAA did not contain the independent records review proposed by the Senate. Senators Schumer and Rounds both vowed at the end of the first session of the 118th Congress to bring back this provision left out by House Leadership.[210] They were left out primarily at the urging of the new Speaker and the Chairs of the House Armed Services and Intelligence Committees. House rank-and-file members would have likely approved the independent review procedure. Overall, except

---

[210] https://www.c-span.org/video/?c5097966/user-clip-schumerrounds-uap-disclosure-act.

for this one item, bipartisanship on the subject of UAP continued in both houses.

The recent bipartisan activity has shown that oversight efforts, mostly behind closed doors, are bearing fruit. Whistleblower accounts have changed the UAP study narrative. NASA unclassified studies and DoD delaying tactics will become meaningless if the proposed UAP legislation finds what it is looking for. If adopted in 2023, this scenario may play out before the 2025 federal fiscal year. If adopted in 2024, the scenario may not play out until the end of 2026. All depends on the level of cooperation Congress receives. Congress will be guided by the "appropriate" national security committees. Each will need to plan how to approach these issues. Each will have to continue to impress upon the service branches and agencies they oversee that the time for transparency has come. Congress must be given all information, good or bad, to help them navigate these unknown waters. Most of these steps will take place behind classified walls. However, when basic information finally enters the public domain, Americans must be able to trust what they hear and see. Having a well-planned process is critical. Picking the correct lane to travel this road is in everybody's best interest.

INDEX

on National Security, the
Border, and Foreign Affairs, 28
Huffington Post, 176
Hynek, Dr. J. Allen, 81-82, 90-91,
98, 100, 118

Infeld, Leopold, 83
Inspector General, 29, 33, 214
Intelligence Advisory Committee,
77, 79
Intelligence Authorization Act, 7,
213, 231
intercontinental ballistic missile
(ICBM), 3, 106
International Geophysical Year, 88
ionosphere, 86, 88
Iran, 58, 62
Italy, 59

Japan Air Lines (JAL), 173, 191
Johns Hopkins Applied Physics
Laboratory, 91
Johns Hopkins University, 81, 89,
91
Joint Army, Navy, Air Force
protocol (JANAP-146), 136, 138-
139

Kelsey Museum of Archeology, 89
Kennedy, John F., 104
Keyhoe, Donald, 129, 154-155
KGB (Committee for State Security,
57, 205
Kirkpatrick, Sean, 18, 20, 24, 26,
27, 30-34, 38-42, 222, 231
Korea, 60-61
Korean War, 90, 148

Lay, James, Jr., 80

Lehigh University, 90
Leslie, Desmond, 129, 157
Lewis, Charles Erwin, 115, 123
Life Magazine, 126, 144
LinkedIn, 30, 41
Lorenzen, Coral, 144
Lorenzen, James, 144
Los Alamos Laboratory, 84
Los Angeles, 105, 120, 125-127,
187, 220
Lundahl, Arthur, 104, 140, 162

Maelstrom Air Force Base, 20
Majestic 12 (MJ-12), 87, 198-200,
202-203
Manhattan Project, 88, 196
Mantell, Thomas, 47, 49
Mao Zedong, 60
Mariana, Nick, 96, 160-161, 167
Marshall Islands, 171
mass psychology, 107, 136, 146
Massachusetts Institute of
Technology (MIT), 69-70, 75, 84,
88
McCarthy, Joseph, 60, 226
McDonald, James E., 118-119
microwave early warning system,
84
Millikan, Max, 75
MK-Ultra, 58, 63, 189
Montana, 96, 97, 161, 167
Montgomery, Alabama, 48, 139
Moultrie, Ronald, 18-20, 24

National Aeronautical Association
(NAA), 126
National Aeronautics and Space
Administration (NASA), 89, 227,
229, 231-232

National Archives and Records
Administration (NARA), 199,
200-202
National Aviation Reporting Center
on Anomalous Phenomenon
(NARCAP), 140
National Defense Authorization Act
(NDAA), 2, 4-5, 8-10, 17
National Defense Research
Committee (NDRC), 86
National Geospatial-Intelligence
Agency (NGA), 29, 214
National Press Club, 2, 20
National Reconnaissance Office
(NRO), 214
National Security Act (Public Law
80-253 (effective July 26,
1947)), 55-56, 94
National Security Council, 69, 71,
73, 76, 80
National Security Resources Board,
115, 123
Naval Air Rocket Test Station, 90
Naval Photo Interpretation
Laboratory, 97, 104, 108, 140,
222
Naval Research Laboratory, 89
near miss, 19, 21-22, 28, 221
New York Times, 1, 15, 26, 156-
157, 221
Newark Star-Ledger, 138
Newhouse, Delbert (D.C.), 96, 160,
162
Nixon, Richard, 18, 156
Nobel Prize, 84
North American Aerospace
Defense Command (NORAD),
180-183

North American Aviation, 105, 125-
126, 191, 220
North Atlantic Treaty Organization
(NATO), 83-84, 88
North Korea, 61, 148
Northwestern University, 88, 91
Nuclear Regulatory Commission
(NRC), 6

Oak Ridge National Laboratories,
196
Odarenko, Todos M., 129, 153, 194
Office of National Estimates (ONE),
114, 219
Office of Naval Intelligence (ONI),
18
Office of Scientific Intelligence
(OSI), 63, 68, 70, 77, 113, 129,
174, 219-220
Office of Scientific Research and
Development (OSRD), 86
Office of Special Investigations
(AFOSI), 161, 163-164, 166, 181,
205, 218
Office of Strategic Services (OSS),
56-57, 62
Office of the Director of National
Intelligence (ODNI), 1, 16, 22,
23, 25, 42-43, 45, 198
Ohio State University, 81-91
Operation Paperclip, 126-127
Orange County, California, 179
Orange County, Claifornia, 179,
181, 183
Oxford University, 89

Pacific Proving Grounds, 171
Page, Dr. Thornton, 80-81, 89, 94-
95

Printed in the USA
CPSIA information can be obtained
at www.ICGtesting.com
JSHW040323160324
59107JS00011B/22/J